THE MEDAL

DODD, MEAD & COMPANY

NEW YORK

1962

NAVY

FRANK DONOVAN

THE MEDAL

THE STORY OF THE MEDAL OF HONOR

ARMY

Grateful acknowledgment is made for the use of material from the
following publications:

Adapted from *They Were Expendable,* copyright, 1942, by W. L.
White. Used by permission of Harcourt, Brace & World, Inc.

The Story of Wake Island by James P. S. Devereux. Published 1947
by J. B. Lippincott Company.

Printed in the United States of America

TO MY SONS
BOB AND MIKEY
AND KEVIN

CONTENTS

THE MEDAL

1

BEYOND THE CALL OF DUTY

As THE GLEAMING WHITE BUILDINGS came into view on the seven distant hills, Fabius became impatient. His chariot had been creeping along at the head of his plodding legions. Now that Rome was in sight he could not wait. He nudged his chariot driver. The long whip cracked. The horses broke into a gallop.

Speeding along the Appian way, clinging to the hand hold on the side of the chariot, he rehearsed his speech. Messengers had gone ahead with news of his victory over Hannibal. He knew that he would receive the highest honors when he reached Rome. He wanted to be ready— to make a good impression on the Senate and the people.

The plunging white horses raced past the temple of Mars a mile from the city wall. Fabius drew himself erect. The cheering people were already crowding the sides of the road. Fabius ignored them, staring straight ahead with the proud dignity that was fitting for a victorious Roman general. The chariot swept through the city gate, slowed to permit lictors to run ahead and force a path through the pressing crowd. The driver added to the excitement by making the horses rear as he pulled the chariot to a halt in front of the forum.

A unit of the Praetorian Guard snapped smartly to attention. Fabius stepped down from the chariot, removed his crested helmet, placed it in the crook of his left arm. He marched proudly into the forum, past the standing senators in their white togas, up to the dais where the consuls waited him. There were speeches. Then a consul stepped forward and placed a wreath made from small branches of laurel on Fabius's head.

This was the first Medal of Honor. It was not worth anything in money. But it was the greatest award that any Roman could win, because it meant that he was the best, the most outstanding, man in his field. It was not given only to brave generals. A man could win it for making a great speech, or writing a great play, or for winning a race. At the Olympic games, the winner is still crowned with a laurel wreath.

As a badge of honor, the laurel wreath had one great fault—it did not last very long. It withered in a few days. Fabius, if he could afford it, would hasten to the nearest sculptor and have a marble statue made of his head with the wreath on it to stand in his living room. His wife could show her envious friends and his children could show their playmates that daddy had been honored beyond all Romans.

The coins of the day were decorated with the Emperor's head, and usually he was wearing a laurel wreath. As time passed, the wreath was moved off the head and placed around the edge of the coin. If you look closely at the back of an American penny, you will see two small branches coming up from the bottom. They are what is left of the laurel wreath after 2,000 years.

To replace the laurel wreath with something that would last, something that a man could wear to show that he had won high honors, metal medals came into being. The first were large coins with the laurel wreath engraved around the edge.

Down through the years the medal has remained the highest symbol of honor and bravery. But for centuries medals were given only to men of high station—kings and princes and noblemen and knights. Every order of knighthood had a medal to identify its members. If King Arthur's knights really existed, they probably wore a medal that showed they were members of the Round Table. The Knights of the Golden Fleece wore one, as did the Knights Templars, the Knights of Jerusalem, and all the other knights of the Crusades.

Nobody ever thought of giving a medal to a common man, to the serfs and peasants who bent their bows and thrust their pikes in the infantry that backed up the knights. In most cases, these were the men who won the battles. But honor was something that only wellborn men were supposed to have, so there was no badge of honor for the common man, no matter how brave he was.

It is quite natural that the first award of honor for the

common soldier was given in the United States, where the conception that all men are equal is fundamental to the way of life. The idea came from George Washington, who issued an order in 1782 that any soldier who showed outstanding bravery—

"—shall be permitted to wear on his left breast the figure of a heart in purple cloth or silk edged with narrow lace. . . . The road to glory is thus opened to all."

The order went on to say that any man who wore the Purple Heart could pass any sentry whom an officer could pass. Only three Purple Hearts were awarded, then it was dropped.

In France, Napoleon Bonaparte picked up the idea. Napoleon knew that he needed something more than brave generals to conquer all of Europe. He needed soldiers who would fight to the death, soldiers who would bravely face overwhelming odds and never give up, soldiers who would be loyal to him in any cause. To instill this kind of bravery and loyalty, he established the French Legion of Honor, a medal for bravery that could be won by a marshal of France, a grenadier in the rear rank, or a saber-swinging dragoon regardless of his station in life.

Soon other countries followed his example. In England there was the Victoria Cross; in Germany, the Iron Cross; in Russia, the Cross of St. George. In the United States there was nothing—no symbol to mark the brave men who risked or gave their lives in the defense of their country.

In addition to the three Purple Hearts, six special medals were awarded during the Revolution, three to generals and three to privates. George Washington got one for beating the British at Boston. General Gates got one for winning the Battle of Saratoga. "Light Horse" Harry Lee, father of General Robert E. Lee, got one for a battle at Paulus Hook, N. J. The other three went to militia men who captured the British spy, Major André, carrying the plans of West Point, which he had received from Benedict Arnold.

Except for these medals, no recognition was given to the hundreds of brave men in the Revolution, in the War of 1812, in the Mexican war, and in the early wars with the Indians in the west. They were unsung heroes, because most people felt that medals were not proper for Americans. They said, "If European soldiers wear medals it's a good reason why American soldiers should not. We want no kings, no knights, no nobles—and no medals. Medals are not democratic."

It was not until 1862, a year after the Civil War had started, that Congress decided this was wrong. One senator said, "Honor is something that no real soldier likes to talk about. Those that want to honor him should provide him with a token that he can wear without words." So Congress passed two bills creating Medals of Honor, one for the Army and one for the Navy. These medals are often called Congressional Medals of Honor, but the correct name is simply Medal of Honor.

The Medal of Honor is not given for ordinary bravery. Fighting men are expected to be brave. That is part of their duty. The Medal of Honor is given only to the bravest of the brave. It is given for:

"—a deed of personal bravery or self sacrifice above and beyond the call of duty while a member of the armed forces in actual combat with an enemy of the nation."

Today, there are other medals for bravery: the Distinguished Service Cross, the Distinguished Service Medal, the Silver Star, the Legion of Merit, the Soldiers Medal, and the revived Purple Heart all form a pyramid of awards for bravery in varying degrees, with the Medal of Honor at the very top of the pyramid.

The Medal of Honor is not worn pinned to the chest like other medals. It is hung around the neck on a blue star-studded ribbon. Few Medal winners ever wear the actual Medal. They think that to do so would be showing off. Instead, they wear a little cloth bar or cloth rosette that reveals they have won the Medal. If you ever see a man in uniform who has a short bar of light-blue silk with five white stars on his left breast, or if you see a man in civilian clothes who has a rosette of light-blue silk with thirteen white stars in the lapel of his coat, you are looking at one of the bravest men you will ever see. This man has won the Medal of Honor.

Along with the greatest honor his country can give him, he gets two dollars a month extra pay (if he is not an officer), a pension of $120 a year when he retires, and the right to travel sometimes on a military plane. But he did not risk his life for two dollars or a free ride in an airplane. He did it because his honor compelled it. As a brave man he could not do less.

Although the Medal did not come into being until the Civil War, the first brave act for which it was awarded took place two months before the war started. It happened out in what is now the State of Arizona.

A band of Apache Indians, led by a young chief named Cochise, swooped down on the isolated ranch of one of the few settlers in the remote region. The settlers' cattle were guarded by their small son. The Indians stole the cattle and kidnaped the boy, to hold him for ransom. Driving the cattle before them, they rode off into the mountains.

The boy's father galloped to Fort Breckenridge, the nearest Army post, for help. Sixty soldiers, commanded by Lieutenant George Bascom, were sent to recover the boy and the cattle. They went to the ranch and easily followed the trail of the Indians and the cattle into the mountains. They caught up with Cochise and a few Indians on a small plain surrounded by mountain peaks.

Bascom rode up to Cochise. "Where is the boy that you took from the ranch?" he said.

"What boy?" replied Cochise. "I know nothing of any boy."

"You lie," said Bascom. "You stole cattle and kidnaped a boy. We have followed your tracks from the ranch. We have come to take them back."

"There is no boy here and no cattle," said Cochise.

"Then we'll take you back and hold you until you tell us where you have them hidden," said Bascom.

"You are a fool to come into my country with so few men," shouted Cochise. "You will never get back to the fort alive. My braves will kill you all."

With this, Cochise swung his pony around and galloped toward the hills, his men streaking after him. This was the signal for the main force of Indians, hidden on the hill-sides, to open fire. Bascom had walked into a trap. He was pinned down on the plain without cover, surrounded by a vastly stronger force of Indians.

The Indians were afraid to charge the little band of soldiers. Instead they tried to pick off men at long range. Since not many of them were armed with rifles, and these were poor marksmen, they succeeded only in wounding a few men. The soldiers held them off until dark. Then Lieutenant Bascom sent a messenger to try to sneak through the Indian lines and bring help from Fort Breckenridge.

The Indians had not posted sentries. They seldom did. Most Indians were afraid of the dark. They thought that evil spirits came out at night, and no Indian wanted to be out alone on sentry duty when evil spirits were around. The messenger had no trouble avoiding the Indians as he crawled over a mountain and streaked back to the fort.

There were not many men left at Fort Breckenridge. Only fourteen could be spared for a relief party. The doctor at the fort, an Irishman named Bernard Irwin, volunteered to lead this small force when he learned that some of Bascom's men had been wounded. The party set out on mules through a blinding blizzard.

Irwin was trained as a doctor, but he was also a smart officer. He would not join Bascom in the trap. He halted his small party as he neared the ring of mountains that sheltered the Indians. Dismounting, he crept forward with two scouts to spy out the lay of the land. Crawling up a ridge behind the Indians, he saw, through the swirling snow, a winding canyon by which he could approach the redskins from the rear.

He sent a man back to bring up the rest of the party. He gave his orders.

"I want absolute quiet as we go up this canyon. When we get near the mouth, there is a place where we can spread out behind the savages. Bugler, you stay with me. When you are all in position, the bugle will sound the charge. Do not charge—I don't want them to know how few of us there are. When the bugle blows, start firing—and yell at the top of your lungs. Try to make a noise like a regiment."

Leaving their mules, the little party, hidden by the falling snow, stole silently through the canyon. When they reached their positions the call of the brazen bugle rang through the hills. In the enclosed canyon it echoed like several bugles. The men fired their carbines, then their pistols, at the same time screaming like madmen.

Irwin's ruse worked. The Indians thought that the whole United States Army was in their rear. They dashed out on the plain, to be caught between the fire of Irwin's men and Bascom's. As their comrades fell under the cross fire, the rest of the Indians panicked and galloped into the hills.

When the two groups of soldiers joined forces, Dr. Irwin took care of the wounded. When he finished this he had done his duty. But Irwin was not the kind of man who was content with merely doing his duty. A white boy was still in the hands of the Indians. It was the Army's job to get him back and punish the Indians. Irwin felt it was up to him to see that the job was done.

Mounting the wounded on the mules, Irwin took command of the joint force. He pushed forward into the hills after the retreating Indians. Crossing the mountain range, he discovered Cochise's village in a valley on the other side. The Indians kept sniping from the flanks at long range, but again they were afraid to make a determined attack. Irwin pushed on to the village.

He found the boy and the cattle. Cochise and his braves galloped in a circle around the village, screaming with rage. Irwin detailed some men to hold them at a distance, others to herd the women and children out of harm's way. Then he burned the village to the ground and started back to the fort with the boy and the cattle, his mission accomplished.

Leading a small force into the heart of Indian country, against an enemy that greatly outnumbered him, was clearly no part of the "duty" of a doctor. When Bernard Irwin risked his life to save a boy and teach the Apaches a much needed lesson, he went far beyond the call of duty. That is why, when he retired from the Army many years later, he was finally awarded the Medal of Honor.

2

DRUMMER BOYS AND GENERALS

Buried in a battle report that crossed Abraham Lincoln's desk was a little paragraph that caught the President's eye. After he read it he picked up his pen and wrote an order.

"By direction of the President let a Medal of Honor be presented to William H. Horsfall, drummer, Company G, First Kentucky Infantry for most distinguished gallantry in action at Corinth Mississippi on the 21st of May 1862. This soldier, a boy of fourteen years of age, voluntarily advanced between two fires and saved the life of an officer who was wounded and lying between the lines."

William Horsfall's duty as a drummer was to stay near his captain and drum out commands. In the infantry, drums were used as well as bugles to signal the charge or retreat. The Captain ordered a charge, then started for-

ward at the head of his men. As Horsfall beat out the command, the Captain fell, wounded, between the Union and
Confederate lines. Horsfall dropped his drum, dashed forward into the enemy fire, with bullets from his own comrades whizzing past his back. Ignoring rifle bullets and
mortar shells, Horsfall dropped to his knees beside his
wounded captain. He slowly crawled back to the Union
lines, pulling his stricken commander to safety.

William Horsfall was the youngest boy to win the Medal
of Honor—but not by much. There were many other soldiers in the Civil War too young to shave but not too
young to be brave beyond the call of duty. "Jennie" Lang-
bein, of the New York Infantry, was one. He was fifteen
when he won his Medal of Honor. His name wasn't Jennie; it was Julius. He had a girl named Jennie back home,
and he was foolish enough to show his comrades a letter
from her. After that, to tease him, he was Jennie to the
older men in his company until he proved that he was
anything but a sissy.

Julius was a drummer, too, and the first part of his brave
act was much like Horsfall's. A comrade was wounded in
the neck. Julius rushed through a rain of bullets, of screaming shot and shell, and carried him to the rear. When he
got to the first-aid station the doctors said that the
wounded man was too near dead; they were too busy to
bother with him. But Julius was stubborn as well as brave.
He dragged the man to the shelter of a house and stayed
with him when the Union forces retreated, leaving them
in the path of the advancing Confederates.

Julius found a wagon and a sorry, starving mule. When

night fell he heaved his unconscious comrade into the wagon and made his way through the Confederate lines, across the battlefield, and through his own lines until he found a doctor who would pay some attention to him. The wounded man lived to see Julius get his Medal of Honor.

Private Delano Morey, of the Ohio Infantry, was older. After the war he wrote a letter telling how he won his Medal. He said:

"Noticing two of the enemy at some distance from me, I left the retreating men and made for the two sharpshooters with the intention of capturing them. When they saw me coming on the full run they hastened to load their guns, but I was a little too quick for them, and, leveling my empty gun at them I ordered them to surrender which they promptly did. When I took them to the colonel he patted me on the head and said, 'You are a good soldier.' I was then sixteen years old."

At the other end of the scale from the boy Medal winners were the grizzled veterans. Major General D. E. Sickles was one. He commanded the Third Corps at Gettysburg. These Union troops bore the brunt of Confederate General Longstreet's charge.

As Sickles watched the gray warriors surge across the fields he was hit in the knee by grapeshot and knocked off his horse. The word ran along the Union line, "The General is dead." The line started to fall back. If Sickles's troops broke, Longstreet could destroy the left flank of the Union Army and get behind it.

In great pain, Sickles called for stretcher bearers. They started to carry him to the rear.

"No," cried Sickles. "Put a blanket over my legs so that

the men can't see how badly I'm hurt. Put a cigar in my mouth and light it. Now carry me along the line so that I can talk to the men and cheer them on."

Led by their general on a stretcher, puffing a cigar to hide his pain, the Third Corps rallied and drove Longstreet back. That night, after the fighting was done, the doctors cut off Sickles's leg.

Brigadier General O. O. Howard also got his Medal for leading his troops after he was wounded. At the Battle of Fair Oaks, while charging at the head of his brigade, he was hit in the right arm by a mini ball. Shifting his sword to his left hand, he kept going. Another bullet smashed his right elbow. Still he kept on at the head of his men until the battle was over.

That night, while the surgeons were amputating Howard's arm, General Phillip Kearney came around to see how he was. Kearney had lost his left arm in Mexico. Howard looked up at him and said, "Well, General, now we can save money on gloves. We can use one pair between us."

In all, there were 2,438 Medals of Honor awarded during the Civil War, more than five times as many as for any other war. After the war, a committee of Congress reviewed the awards and canceled 911 of them, calling the Medals back because they did not think the heroism involved was great enough to warrant the Medal.

There were several reasons why so many Medals were awarded. First, there were then no other medals for lesser bravery—it was either the Medal of Honor or nothing. Also when the Medal first came into being, many commanding officers did not understand that it was only for bravery "beyond the call of duty." The Medal was given to some men who were not entitled to it—men who were brave, but whose bravery was not great enough to earn the cherished Medal.

But the main reason why the Civil War resulted in so many Medals was not either of these. This war of Americans against Americans, of neighbor against neighbor, sometimes of brother against brother, seemed to call out the utmost in courage and self-sacrifice. Also the type of fighting gave more opportunity for acts of individual valor to stand out than in more recent wars.

The Civil War was different from any war before or since. It was a "turning point" war. Some of the tactics and weapons were as old as armies; some represented the birth of modern warfare. Rifles, accurate to 500 yards, had replaced muskets, which were accurate only by luck beyond fifty yards. The revolver had replaced the pistol, the repeating carbine came into use, and the machine gun had been born—invented by a Dr. Gatling for humane reasons. He hated war and killing. He thought his rapid-fire gun would kill men so fast that it would make war too horrible and there would be no more wars.

Despite these new weapons, the biggest cavalry battle of American history, Brandy Station, was fought almost entirely with swinging sabers in the manner of knights of olden days.

There were new tactics. Trenches and foxholes were used extensively for the first time, particularly by the Confederates. Yet much of the fighting involved marching upright across an open field in the face of the enemy. There was less creeping and crawling than in modern war, more running and charging.

The Battle of Gettysburg is an example of a mixture of the old and the new. When General Pickett made his famous charge on Cemetery Ridge, his men marched across the valley and up the hill in regimental front. When Union rifles and massed artillery tore gaps in the line, the men closed in and marched on, following their flag. Eighty-seven years before, the British Redcoats had used exactly the same tactics at the Battle of Bunker Hill.

On another part of the same battlefield, Confederate infantry was holed up among the rocks in Devil's Den, pouring a withering fire into the Union forces on Little Round Top in an action very much like the "fire fights" of the recent war in Korea.

Regardless of weapons and tactics, most Civil War battles ended in hand-to-hand fighting with bayonets, knives, clubbed rifles, rocks, and fists. Here, everybody fought, from privates to generals, and the flag was most important. Today a fighting man in a plane, at a rocket-launching site, or buttoned up in a tank may fight for days without seeing the Stars and Stripes. It was not so in the Civil War.

Then the flag was the focal point of every fight. Men followed it anywhere as long as it waved. When it was lost, they often retreated. When the flag bearer was shot down others willingly vied for the dangerous honor of carrying the colors. Men willingly gave their lives to protect their piece of bunting or to shame the enemy by capturing his. This report from one colonel shows what happened in most battles.

"I cannot omit an account in this report of the color guard. Color Sergeant Doolittle fell early in the engagement, pierced by four balls and dangerously wounded. The colors were taken by Corporal Page who soon fell dead. They were again raised by Corporal Churcher who had his arm broken as he entered the entrenchments; when they were taken by Corporal Twombley who was almost immediately knocked down by a spent ball. He got up and bore them gallantly to the end of the fight."

Corporal Twombley won the Medal of Honor.

Both the first and last brave acts in the Civil War that won Medals had to do with capturing the Confederate flag. The first stirred up the people of the North almost as much as the firing on Fort Sumter.

There was a young man named Elmer Ellsworth. He was a colonel in the militia—had been a colonel almost since he was old enough to vote. He had raised a company of Zouaves in Chicago, trained them as a crack drill team, and toured the country with them. People turned out by the thousands to see them and to honor the handsome young colonel with banquets, gift swords, and armfuls of roses.

Zouaves got their name from their gaudy uniform, which consisted of baggy, bright-red pants, short white leggings, a short blue coat with yellow and orange trimming, and a little red hat. Originally, this had been the uniform of a unit of French troops recruited in Algeria from a Berber tribe called Zouaves.

President Lincoln was very fond of Ellsworth and treated him almost like a son. The President once said, "He is the greatest little man I ever knew." When Lincoln came to Washington for his inauguration, Ellsworth came with him, and an order was given that "The President elect will not attempt to pass through any crowd until such arrangements have been made that will meet the approval of Colonel Ellsworth." Lincoln's trip was considered dangerous. There were many Southern sympathizers who might attempt to kill him. The one man he relied on more than all others was young Colonel Ellsworth.

After Ellsworth got Lincoln safely to Washington he went to New York and raised another regiment of Zouaves from members of the New York Fire Department. A month after the war started, Ellsworth brought his Zouaves to Washington. The visiting firemen made it hot for the Capital. They were high-spirited young men with strange ideas of what was fun. Quartered in a tall warehouse, they did not bother to use the stairs. They hung ropes from the roof, and when they wanted to go out, they jumped out the windows and slid to the ground.

Many of them charged meals that they ordered in hotels to the Confederate government, saying they would go South and collect. One of their favorite sports was playing tag on the unfinished dome of the Capitol building, racing around the very edge of the parapet two hundred feet from the ground.

They somewhat redeemed themselves with the people of Washington when the city's principal hotel, Willard's, caught fire. The New York firemen raced to the scene. Some of them formed a human pyramid, standing on each other's shoulders to reach people in upstairs windows and pass them down to safety. Others formed a human chain from the roof, hanging their comrades by the heels to shoot a hose into lower windows.

Washington heaved a sigh of relief when the Zouaves boarded a transport to sail down the Potomac and capture the Confederate-held town of Alexandria, Virginia. When they arrived, the Confederate forces had left, and the town was ready to surrender. As Colonel Ellsworth walked along the main street of the captured town he was amazed to see, flying from the roof of a small hotel, the Confederate Stars and Bars. He rushed into the hotel, followed by a corporal named Francis Brownell.

In the front room of the hotel they found a man, his bare feet propped on a table, reading a newspaper.

"What is that flag doing on the roof?" shouted Ellsworth.

"I don't know anything about it," replied the man. "I'm only a boarder here."

Ellsworth, still followed by Brownell, raced up the stairs to the third floor, found a ladder, and climbed to the roof. He cut down the flag, put it under his arm, and the two men started down. As they reached the middle of the first flight, the barefoot man from the front room, who was really the owner of the hotel, stepped out of the shadows with a double-barreled shotgun. Without saying a word, he fired the first barrel into Ellsworth's chest, killing him instantly.

Ellsworth fell and rolled down the stairs. The hotel owner leveled the gun at Brownell. As he pulled the trigger on the second barrel, Brownell leaped down to the landing, knocked the barrel aside, and shot him in the

face. Then, to make sure, he plunged his bayonet into
the dead hotel owner's chest.

The entire Union went into mourning for Ellsworth,
and Brownell was awarded the Medal of Honor. The
award was prompted more by the people's love for Ellsworth than by Brownell's brave action. What he did was
not "beyond the call of duty." Actually, he fired in self-
defense.

The last act of the Civil War for which a Medal was
awarded, and which resulted in the capture of another
Confederate flag, was clearly beyond the call of duty.

It was at a little battle at Sailor's Creek, Virginia. Company H of the First West Virginia Cavalry had charged the
Confederate earthworks. It was a foolish thing to do, for
cavalry were seldom successful attacking entrenched infantry. But their general, George Armstrong Custer, was
watching, and the men wanted to win his praise.

As the line of horsemen galloped forward, they presented grand targets for the Confederates hidden behind
their earthen parapet. One trooper after another went
down until only five men of the company were left. They
crouched for shelter behind the bodies of dead horses—
except for one man, Sergeant Francis Cunningham.

Cunningham's horse had been shot from under him.
Nearby he spied a Confederate mule running around the
battlefield, mad with excitement. As the mule dashed past,
Cunningham grabbed his bridle, swung on his back, and
turned his head toward the Confederate line. The crazed
animal galloped straight for the enemy works and scrambled up the breastworks in front of the Confederate flag.
Cunningham tore the flag from the hands of the Confed-

erate color sergeant, wrenched the mule's head around, and galloped back to his own lines, the Stars and Bars floating over his head. By a miracle he was untouched by the hail of bullets that followed him.

Three days later General Lee surrendered at Appomattox. General Custer sent Cunningham to Washington to present the last Confederate flag captured in battle to Secretary of War Stanton. On the spot, Stanton awarded Cunningham the Medal of Honor.

The Union Navy in the Civil War had its share of Medal of Honor winners—327 of them. Fourteen of these Medals went to a crew of volunteers who sank a Confederate ironclad warship with a little steam launch.

The ironclad *Albermarle* was a flat-bottomed boat with an iron fort, mounting two guns, built on it. The Confederates had built it in a cornfield out of scrap iron, launched it in the Roanoke River in North Carolina, and sent it out to fight the Union fleet that was blockading the mouth of the river.

The *Albermarle* wasn't much of a warship, but it was an ironclad. The Union ships were far bigger, but they were made of wood. The *Albermarle* first fought two of them, sank one. She then fought nine of them and put one out of action. The others pulled off when they found that their shells exploded harmlessly against the *Albermarle*'s iron sides. The *Albermarle* steamed back up the river, helped the Confederate Army capture the town of Plymouth, and anchored eight miles from the river's mouth.

The Union Navy had to put the *Albermarle* out of action if they were to keep up the blockade that was preventing the Confederates from getting guns and supplies from abroad. Lieutenant William Cushing offered to go up the river and try to torpedo it.

The torpedo of the Civil War was nothing like the torpedo of today. It was a keg or can of gunpowder that would explode when it was pushed against the side of a ship. It was mounted on a long pole which stuck out from the bow of a rowboat or small launch. The small boat carrying the torpedo would sneak up to a big ship, lower the torpedo under water, and drive it against the vessel's side. Men who volunteered for duty on a torpedo boat seldom came back if their mission was successful, for the torpedo usually sank the boat that was carrying it as well as the ship it was supposed to sink.

Thirteen brave men volunteered to go with Cushing. In the middle of a moonless night they dropped into a small steam launch. The torpedo, a large copper can filled with gunpowder, was carried on a pole that stood in the bow. When and if they reached the *Albermarle* the pole would be lowered by ropes to stick out in front of the boat.

They approached the mouth of the narrow river. Cushing called his men to the stern. He told them, "The Confederates surely have sentries on the banks of the river. Our only hope is that they will be watching the fleet and not the river—they don't expect an attack from here. We'll go dead slow to keep the engine quiet and avoid sparks from the stack. When you have to put wood in the firebox, make a shield with your coats to cover the glare."

Slowly the little boat crept up the river, the men holding their breaths as they waited a hail from the shore. None came. For two hours they groped their way upstream through the darkness. Then a glow appeared in the sky. As they rounded a bend in the river they saw the *Albermarle* ahead. The glow was from a fire on shore. It lit up the *Albermarle*—and an alert lookout on her deck.

And they saw something else. The *Albermarle* was tied to a wharf. Surrounding her, the Confederates had built a boom of logs floating on the water and chained together. Nothing could get within fifty feet of the *Albermarle,* and their torpedo pole was only twenty-eight feet long.

Cushing stopped the boat outside the glare of the fire and called a whispered conference.

"We've come too far to turn back," he said. "If we hit the log boom hard I think we may ride over it. Open the draft, get the fire hot, and lay low."

From the deck of the *Albermarle* the sentry saw a shower of sparks from the stack of the launch as the draft was opened.

"Who's there?" he called.

There was no answer.

"What boat is that?" he called again.

Then as the launch came into the edge of the firelight, he screamed, "All hands!"

The crew of the *Albermarle* tumbled from their hammocks, dashed to the guns. The launch came on, gathering speed. It hit the log boom. The bow went up in the air, pushing a log under water. The launch shuddered for a moment. Then it grated over the log.

"Lower the torpedo!" cried Cushing.

As the torpedo splashed into the water, the *Albermarle*'s bow gun sent a load of grapeshot whistling around the approaching launch. A man at Cushing's side fell, wounded, but the gun was not well aimed by the half-awake gunners. The launch came on.

Before the gun could be reloaded the torpedo crashed into the *Albermarle*'s side. The mighty explosion tore a hole in the *Albermarle* below the water line and sent a huge wave back to swamp the launch. As the little boat went under, the crew leaped into the river. Marksmen on the slowly sinking *Albermarle* fired at their bobbing heads without effect in the dark.

Cushing swam under water as long as he could. When he came up he was alone, some distance down the river. He saw a boat from the *Albermarle* pick up some of his comrades. He continued swimming downstream for half a mile, and then, exhausted, he dragged himself out on the bank and crawled into the swamp.

When he had regained his strength, Cushing plunged into the dense swamp to escape the sentries on the bank. He fought his way through mud and slime in the dark, fighting off mosquitoes and snakes, until he came to a small creek, which he followed cautiously back to the river. Here luck favored him. He found an unguarded enemy picket boat. Paddling with his hands, he floated down to the mouth of the river, where he was picked up by a Union gunboat.

One other member of the launch's crew escaped. The bodies of two who were drowned were picked up the next day. The other ten spent the rest of the war in a Confederate prison—consoled, perhaps, by the knowledge that they had saved the Union blockade and performed one of the most daring feats in naval history.

3

MEDALS FOR THIEVES

THE FIRST TWENTY MEN who actually received the Medal of Honor were thieves. That's what they got their medals for—stealing. They stole a railroad train.

The Civil War was the first war in which railroads were used. During the quarter century before the war, railroads had been built connecting all the principal Southern cities. Troops and supplies could be moved quickly from place to place by whichever side controlled the railroads. This created a new problem for the generals, one that they had never faced before. In planning battles they had to think about the railroads—how to use their railroads to build up a strong force at a point where the enemy could not use his railroads to bring large numbers against them. The side that controlled a railroad usually commanded the entire area through which the railroad ran. Battles could be won or prevented by capturing or destroying the enemy's railroads.

Destroying railroads became one of the principal jobs of the cavalry. Before the war was very old, the Confederate cavalry had figured out a neat way to do it. They would ride around the flank of the enemy and approach the railroad in the rear of his lines. While some of the troopers fanned out and dismounted to guard against attack, the rest of the horse soldiers ripped up rails and ties. They heaped the wooden ties in piles, poured oil on them, and set them on fire. They laid the rails in the fire. When the centers of the rails got cherry red, two troopers grabbed a rail by each end, ran to the nearest tree, and wrapped it around the trunk of the tree. Then they mounted up and rode off, leaving the useless rails tied in bow knots around the trees.

Out in Tennessee was a Union general named Ormsby Mitchell, who had to destroy a railroad in order to carry out a plan which might bring about the early defeat of the Confederacy. The Union forces occupied western Tennessee. The Confederates were in eastern Tennessee. If General Mitchell could capture the city of Chattanooga from the Confederates, the Union forces would control the entire state, and from Chattanooga they could attack the Confederate Army in Virginia from the rear.

It was a fine plan. It should be easy to capture Chattanooga because the Confederates had only a few troops there. But Chattanooga was connected with Atlanta, Georgia, by the Western and Atlantic Railroad. And the Confederates had many men in Atlanta who could come to the defense of Chattanooga in a few hours on the trains.

At Mitchell's headquarters was a civilian named James Andrews. Quiet, soft-spoken, well-mannered, he seemed like a man who might be a teacher, a writer, or a minister. Andrews was none of these. He was one of the best Union spies. He spent most of his time behind the Confederate lines gathering information on the Southerner's plans, which he brought back to Union generals.

Mitchell and Andrews put their heads together. They came up with a scheme for destroying the railroad that might work because it was so foolhardy, so daring, that the Confederates would never suspect it. To make it work would call for all of Andrews's cool skill as a secret agent, and a group of reckless, fearless men.

Mitchell called for volunteers from among his soldiers. He did not tell them what he wanted them to do. He said he wanted men to go on a dangerous mission behind the enemy lines in civilian clothes. The men knew that meant certain death if they were caught. By the rules of war a soldier behind the enemy lines in civilian clothes is treated as a spy and hanged. Many men volunteered.

Andrews carefully selected twenty-two men—including some who had experience at railroading before they joined the army. He told them the plan.

"We're going behind the enemy line all the way to Marietta, Georgia," he said. "When we get there we're going to steal a railroad train. We're going to drive that train back to Chattanooga, destroying the railroad behind us as we go. Now that you know what you're up against, does anybody want to back out? Nobody will blame you if you do, because the end of this may well be a Confederate bullet or a rope."

Nobody spoke.

"Very well," said Andrews. "We'll start now. Break up

into groups of two or three. Get through the Cumberland Mountains and across the Tennessee River on foot. When you cross the river you'll be in enemy country. Go on into Chattanooga, walk boldly into the railroad station, and buy tickets for Marietta. Meet me in the hotel in Marietta not later than Thursday night."

"Wait a minute," said a soldier. "How are we going to get through the enemy lines without being stopped by their sentries?"

"You probably won't," said Andrews. "When you're challenged, tell the sentry that you're from Kentucky and that you are on your way to Chattanooga to join the Confederate Army."

Kentucky was not in the Confederacy, but many Kentuckians were Southern sympathizers who came down to Tennessee to join the Confederates.

"What if they call our bluff and want us to join their army on the spot?" asked another soldier.

"Join it," replied Andrews. "That's better than giving our plan away and getting hung. You can escape back to our lines the first time you're on picket duty. If there are no more questions let's get going. Good luck. I'll see you in Marietta."

For three days the little groups of daredevils made their way cross-country to Chattanooga. Some slept in barns and haystacks. Some boldly asked for shelter from farmers and at inns. Most of these found that their story of being from Kentucky worked very well. The Southerners gave them the best of everything—nothing was too good for these brave Kentuckians who had come to help the Southern cause.

Two of the men did not make out so well. When they told their story at an inn, a Confederate officer stepped forward and said, "If you want to join the Army you don't have to go to Chattanooga. I'll swear you in right here." And he did.

By Thursday night all but these two had arrived at the hotel in Marietta. Andrews gathered them in his room and explained the rest of the plan.

He said, "At five-thirty tomorrow morning we'll board the mail train from Atlanta going north. That's the train we're going to steal. Stay in the groups that you traveled in. Each group will buy tickets to a different station so that they won't think we are together. Everybody is to ride in the first car, but don't let on that you know each other.

"Eight miles up the line is a place called Big Shanty. The train stops there for twenty minutes so that the passengers and crew can get breakfast. There is no telegraph at Big Shanty, so they can't wire up ahead after we steal the train. When everybody else gets out for breakfast, we'll slip out the other side of the car. The train is made up of three boxcars behind the engine, with two passenger cars behind them. Brown and Knight, you will uncouple the passenger cars and then get on the engine— you used to be railroad engineers. Wilson will ride the engine, too, to feed the fire. The rest of you will get in the last boxcar."

The men went back to their rooms for a few hours' sleep. Andrews did not sleep. Instead, he carefully wrote a letter to himself on a Confederate Army letterhead that he had stolen. The letter said that James Andrews and the men who were with him were on official business, and anybody to whom the letter was presented should help them. He signed it with the name of the South's favorite general, P. G. T. Beauregard.

Next morning the men went to the station, bought their tickets, and boarded the train. They sat quietly until the train reached Big Shanty. When the rest of the passengers got off to have breakfast they slipped out the other side of the train and climbed into a boxcar.

The tracks were guarded by Confederate sentries. Andrews had put on his best clothes. He looked like an important man. The sentries thought that he was an official of the railroad as he boldly ordered his men to uncouple the passenger cars. They watched with interest as he climbed on the locomotive—which was named the *General*—and the head end of the train pulled out.

The conductor of the train was a young man named Fuller. He looked up from his breakfast as he heard the engine start. Shouting, "Somebody's stealing my train," he dashed out of the station, his napkin still tucked under his chin. Followed by the engineer and another man, he ran down the tracks after the speeding train.

In the cab of the locomotive, Andrews relaxed. The hard part of the job was done. A mile from the station the train passed a work gang. The men in the locomotive waved to them. Another mile passed. Thinking they were safe from pursuit, Andrews ordered the train stopped. The men piled out. Two of them climbed telegraph poles and cut out a length of wire. The rest pried up a section of track and threw the rails and ties in the boxcar. The train went on.

Fuller and his two companions were still running along the track.

"We'll never catch them on foot," panted the engineer.

"We'll catch them. They can't get away with stealing my train," replied Fuller.

The work gang that Andrews had passed had a handcar. When the running men reached the gang, Fuller ordered them to put the handcar on the tracks, and the three men jumped aboard, pushing the car forward with a long pole. This section of the line was downhill, and they gathered speed until they reached the section of track that Andrew's men had ripped up. When the handcar hit this it flew into the air, spilling the riders into a ditch. Unhurt, they put the car back on the tracks beyond the break and went on.

Up in the speeding train, Andrews was thinking about his one remaining problem. The railroad was a single-track line. Trains going north had to pull off on a siding to let trains going south pass. Andrews knew that a train from the north was due to pass his train at a town called Kingston. He would have to pull off on the siding at Kingston and wait, or run head-on into the southbound train.

While he was thinking about this the train passed an ironworks where there was a small yard engine on a siding. Andwers scarcely noticed it as the train sped on.

Fuller noticed it. When he reached the ironworks he jumped from the handcar and climbed aboard the yard engine. His companions threw wood into the firebox and soon had steam up. It wasn't much of an engine, but it was better than a handcar. Fuller again took up the chase, many miles behind Andrews and his men.

When Andrews reached Kingston he ran into trouble. The southbound train was late. They would have a long wait on the siding, and the station was full of Confederate soldiers. Still, if he kept calm, they might be all right. While the engine crew made a show of oiling the engine and the men in the boxcar scarcely dared to breathe, Andrews walked back to talk to the station agent. The station agent was full of questions.

"Where's the rest of the train?" he asked. "Where's Fuller?"

Andrews pulled out his letter from "Beauregard" and showed it to the station agent.

"This is an emergency," he said. "They're expecting an attack on Chattanooga. I'm taking up ammunition under orders from Beauregard. Fuller will be along later with the mail and the passengers."

"Is there anything I can do to help?" asked the station agent.

"Just keep everybody away from the train," replied Andrews. "I don't want any accidents."

The station agent posted Confederate guards to keep anybody from interfering with the Union men who were out to wreck his railroad.

To the nervous Union soldiers huddled in the boxcar, not knowing what was going on outside, it seemed like hours before they heard the southbound train pant into the station. As their train pulled off the siding onto the now clear main line, one of them peeked out the back of the boxcar. In the distance he saw a plume of black smoke.

"Look!" he cried. "We're being followed."

When Fuller's little yard engine wheezed into Kingston

he found the track blocked by the southbound train. He rushed into the station shouting, "Where's my train?"

"It left about five minutes ago," said the station agent. "That fellow with orders from Beauregard is taking ammunition to Chattanooga."

"He is not," cried Fuller. "He's stealing my train. They must be deserters. Clear the main line so that I can get through. No, wait a minute."

The southbound train was pulled by a big, new locomotive. the *Texas*. It was more powerful than the yard engine.

Fuller continued. "Push that train on the siding, uncouple the engine, and bring it back on the main line. Give me a squad of soldiers to ride the tender. I'll catch those deserters."

Running backward and bristling with Confederate bayonets, the *Texas* pulled out in pursuit of the *General*.

The track was now clear in front of Andrews all the way to Chattanooga. But knowing that he was being chased, he had a new problem. He had to delay the pursuit to gain time to burn a long wooden bridge over the Chicamaugua River. This would put the railroad out of commission for months.

He stopped the train and ordered his men to tear up another section of track. But fate was against them. The spikes that held the rails to the ties were rusted. As they struggled to loosen a rail the column of smoke from the *Texas* appeared on the horizon. It got bigger and bigger as the pursuing train approached, and still the rail did not give. When the *Texas* was less than a mile away they

gave up and jumped back in their boxcar, having succeeded
in loosening only one end of the rail.

The *General* gathered speed. The men watched breath-
lessly as the *Texas* approached the lose rail, hit it and kept
coming. The Confederate engine had not been derailed.
The chase was still on.

Pursuit was too close for Andrews to stop again. He had
another idea.

"Knock a hole in the back of the last boxcar," he told
the men. "Throw those ties out and try to land them
across the tracks. Maybe that will derail them."

One after another the men threw the ties on the tracks,
watched them bounce off or lie between the rails. When
the last tie was gone the track was still clear.

"Everybody up ahead," said Andrews. "When we reach
the next upgrade we'll uncouple the last boxcar and let it
roll back. That ought to stop them."

As the *Texas* rounded a bend, Fuller saw the boxcar
rolling slowly toward the engine.

"Throw her in reverse!" he shouted.

Sparks flew as the wheels of the *Texas* spun, trying to
grip the track and reverse the engine. The *Texas* started
to move slowly in the same direction as the boxcar. When
they collided there was only a slight bump. Again the
Texas was reversed. It pushed the empty boxcar to the
next siding, shunted it off, and took up the chase.

The delay had been too short to help the Union men,
and they were rapidly approaching the covered bridge
over the Chicamaugua. Andrews had one last hope. He told
his men.

"Get the oil can from the engine. Squirt the oil around

the rear boxcar. We'll set it afire and leave it in the middle of the bridge. By the time they get there the bridge will be burning, and they have no way to put it out."

They left the car blazing brightly on the covered wooden bridge. But luck was still against the Union soldiers. It had rained for days. The wood of the bridge was soaked. When the *Texas* came up, the bridge had not caught fire. As the men on the speeding *General* watched, the flaming boxcar slowly emerged from the end of the bridge, pushed by the *Texas*.

The plan to wreck the railroad had failed. Then Wilson, the fireman, had more bad news. He turned from the fire-box and said, "That's the last of the wood. We can't keep steam up for more than another mile."

As the steam pressure fell, the *General* groaned to a halt. The *Texas* had stopped to shove the burning boxcar on a siding, but she would come on again with her tender full of Confederate troops. The men stood around the silent *General*.

Andrews said, "The only thing we can do is scatter in the woods. Some of us may get around Chattanooga and back to our own lines.

The men walked off into the forest to start their long and dangerous journey.

Meanwhile, the telegraph had been active at Kingston sending word ahead. Troops were rushing down from Chattanooga by train. Cavalry was gathering to surround the area. The Confederates combed the woods, driving the cornered Union men before them into the hands of the waiting cavalry.

All of them were captured. One after another they were

gathered together in a prison in Atlanta. Shackled hand and foot and chained to the walls of their cells, there was nothing more that the brilliant Andrews and his brave volunteers could do.

Andrews and six of the men were tried, condemned, and hung as spies. Before the remainder were brought to trial they staged a daring jail break by opening their manacles with a key that one of them had carved from a bone. Again they tried to reach their lines, and this time eight of them succeeded.

By the time the remaining six were recaptured, the Confederates had changed their minds about hanging them. They could not help but admire these courageous men and decided to treat their exploit as a military mission instead of a spying one. The six men were exchanged for an equal number of Confederate prisoners and sent north.

Back in uniform they went to Washington to report to Secretary of War Stanton and then to President Lincoln. Stanton promoted them to lieutenants and gave each man a bonus of $100. Then picking up a pile of little boxes, he hung the new Medal of Honor around the neck of each man. The other fourteen volunteers, living and dead, were also awarded Medals. No award was made to Andrews. He was a civilian.

Although Medals were later awarded to some men, like Irwin and Brownell, whose brave deeds were done before the railroad raid, these Medals for the "train thieves" were the first to be given out.

4

MEDALS FOR MESSENGERS

ONE INDIAN BRAVE was strutting around in the dark-blue cavalry jacket. Another was pulling the light-blue britches with the yellow stripe over his breechclout. A third threw the boots aside in disgust—they hurt his feet. Meanwhile the squaws had tied the wounded trooper to stakes driven into the ground.

Small boys gathered twigs of sagebrush. Two squaws made a fire under the trooper's right foot. It was a very small fire. It would take a long time to roast the foot. When it did they would build another fire under the left foot, then under one hand, then under the other. Finally, they would build a fire on his chest and keep it burning until he died.

This was the fate of some soldiers who were captured in the wars with the Indians which raged in the West for twenty-five years after the Civil War ended. From Kansas to the Coast, from Canada into Mexico, the little regular Army marched and fought and froze and starved to make the red man's land safe for the greedy white man.

The Indian was desperate. He was fighting for his life—or, at least, his way of life. With weapons from the Stone Age he tried to hold back the railroad, the plow, the "whispering wires" of the telegraph—all of the white man's civilization that was trying to pen him up on reservations of useless land, often to starve. He made treaties with the white man, which the white man broke. When he came off the reservation to fight for his rights, it was up to the Army to catch him, to punish him, to put him back in his pen. The Army had not made the treaties, but they had to enforce them.

Merely serving in the Indian-fighting Army called for endurance "beyond the call of duty." Soldiers fighting the Sioux in the Bad Lands of Dakota and Montana faced cold of sixty degrees below zero. Fighting the Apaches in the Southwest they faced heat that was often more than 130 degrees above. Soldiers called this Indian territory "Hell with the fire out." They told a story about a trooper who died and went to the lower regions. Next night he came back. When they asked him why, he said, "I came for my blankets. It's cold down there."

Water was usually a problem. Many a trooper, pinned down by Indians, drank the blood of his dead horse. Some cut open the veins of their arms and drank their own blood to stay alive a little longer.

Far out on the plains or in the rugged mountains there were none of the refinements of civilized war. When the troops were on patrol, doctors were scarce. One soldier wrote home to tell how he sat on a log and pried out an aching tooth with his penknife.

Being wounded was serious in another way. A wounded soldier separated from his comrades usually saved his last bullet for himself, because capture meant death by Indian torture. If the Indians were in a hurry he might be tied to a wagon wheel and burned to death. If they had more time he might be staked to the ground beside an ant hill, his mouth pried open with a stick and filled with sugar, with a sugar trail leading to the hungry ants.

The Apaches sometimes hung captives head down over a fire. Or they might tie them to a bayonet cactus with wet rawhide, which, when it shrank in the sun, would pull the victim toward the cactus until the sharp spikes ran through him. One horrible but quick practice was to fill a prisoner's mouth with gunpowder and light it.

The least a wounded man could expect was to be scalped before he died. The scalp was the Indian's Medal of Honor. Braves who lifted hair were held in high regard by their tribesmen. White soldiers did their share of scalping, too—particularly state militia. When the 2nd Colorado Cavalry massacred a village of Cheyennes their Colonel came out on the stage of a theater in Denver between the acts of a play to exhibit over one hundred scalps that they had lifted.

The Army usually fought against great odds—anywhere from two to one to twenty-five or more to one. There was some difference of opinion as to how good the Indian was as a fighter. Many people said that most Indians were cowards, but the people who said this were not the people who were doing the fighting. Phil Sheridan, the Union's great cavalry general, said that the plains Indians were the finest light cavalry the world had ever seen.

Even with their greater numbers, the Indians must have been good to hold out so long with bows and arrows, lances, and war clubs against rifles, Gatlings, and "wagon guns," as they called the Army's dreaded artillery. The Indians had some rifles that they captured, bought from traders, and got from the government for hunting on the reservations. But most of the braves did not have firearms, and they never had enough ammunition to learn how to become good marksmen.

During the quarter century between the end of the Civil War and the year 1890 the Indians were good enough fighters to give 416 soldiers opportunities to win the Medal of Honor. These Medals were awarded for all kinds of brave deeds—saving wounded comrades, rescuing white captives, fighting against great odds, and other acts of valor. And because of the nature of the fighting, many of them were given for carrying messages.

Army posts were isolated, many miles apart. Columns in the field ranged far from the posts. Communication over terrain where hostile savages lurked was a difficult and dangerous business. Also small bodies of troops were frequently cut off and surrounded by large bodies of Indians. When this happened they took cover if they could and tried to hold off the redskins until help came. Messengers who volunteered to go through the Indian lines usually took their lives in their hands "beyond the call of duty."

Out in what is now Nebraska was Fort Phillip Kearney, anchor of a chain of posts guarding the new road to Montana. Ninety miles to the west was a smaller outpost, Fort

C. F. Smith. In December, 1866, a wood-cutting party from Fort Kearney was attacked by Sioux. Colonel Fetterman and eighty-four men from the fort went to their relief. The savages withdrew and the wood detail came in as Fetterman pursued the Indians. Fetterman did not come back. Another relief column went out.

They found what was left of Fetterman's force. Strewn around a boulder where they had been ambushed were the horribly mutilated bodies of eighty-five men—eyes torn out, heads, limbs, ears, and noses hacked off, teeth knocked out, and the bodies filled with arrows which the Indian boys had shot into them after the braves finished their butchery. The Sioux were on the warpath in force.

Two months passed. There was no word from Fort C. F. Smith. The regular couriers had stopped coming after the massacre. Two attempts by scouts to reach Smith from Kearney had failed because of deep snow, severe cold, and swarming Sioux. Two sergeants of the Eighteenth Infantry, Joseph Graham and George Grant, volunteered to make a third try to find out if the outpost had been wiped out.

Sergeant Grant came back. When he returned, an unknown company clerk wrote out his report to the company commander of his nine-day walk in the snow.

DEPARTMENT OF THE PLATTE

FORT PHILLIP KEARNEY

February 14th 1867

"Lieutenant: I have the honor to report that about reveille on the morning of the 4th inst., in company with First Sergeant Joseph Graham, Co. G, 18th Infantry, I started for Fort C. F.

Smith. Arriving at the north end of Buried Mountain about noon we could now plainly see the north end of Big Horn Mountain and judged same to be about seventy miles distant, allowing that we had travelled about twenty miles. The snow thus far was very deep but now, over a belt of country some ten miles in extent, there was scarcely any snow at all.

"We travelled all night due north and at daylight northeast for about four miles, and struck the government road at sunrise. After breakfasting we continued on the government road, which we kept all day, wading through large creeks including that of Big Horn. At 3 P.M. we were again troubled with deep snow in the road and were obliged to pass the night on the prairie without fire.

"Feb. 6th: This morning we again found the government road and travelled south. About 4 P.M. there came a tremendous storm of sleet and snow. We lost the road at 8 P.M. and were obliged to pass the night on an open prairie without fire.

"Feb. 7th: At 6 A.M. we stopped and made a fire for the first time. Our feet were in very bad condition. We arrived at Fort C. F. Smith about 4 P.M. where we were warmly received by the officers and here remained the 8th and 9th.

"Feb. 9th: Returning we started about tattoo with the mail accompanied by an Indian guide to whose orders we were now subject. We were each furnished a horse to ride, besides a mule to carry the mail and one to carry forage. We travelled until 4 A.M. on the 10th.

"Feb. 10th: From 9 A.M. until 1 P.M. we travelled briskly, reaching the Little Horn four miles north of the government road. Our horses were well nigh exhausted, we having been running and trotting them all day. The guide now said that there were Indians around and wished to know what to do. I proposed travelling southwest upon the top of a mountain and in case of attack to get in the pine timber as soon as possible. At this proposition the guide abandoned the mail, stripped the mules, threw away his saddle, rations and everything and going upon the crest of a hill said that there were Indians in view and after us on horseback and, taking the lead, started southwesterly for home. We ran our horses about fifteen miles without intermission.

"About 3.30 P.M. Indians, about fifteen in number, came yelling toward us. I told the guide to halt in the pines and we would fight them. My horse being now completely fagged and being dismounted and the Indians in warm pursuit of us I became separated from the others for the balance of the journey.

"I soon discovered a cave, inaccessible on all sides but one. Here I sat down and could hear the Indians after the balance of the party, yelling like demons. Here I remained, prepared against attack, the sun only about half an hour high. One Indian presently came down, dressed in buckskins, a Henry rifle in his hand. Upon seeing him I fired. He yelled and dropped his rifle on the bank, jumped the precipice and fell dead. At sundown there was a young Indian came up upon whom I also fired. He jumped and, falling dead over a precipice, hung on a pine.

"About this time there came from the east a heavy white fog, enveloping everything. I here turned to peep out of the cave, over the edge of the hill and, seeing no Indians in view, travelled the same way they did for about fifty yards, struck bare ground, and travelled nearly south all night.

"Feb. 11th: At daylight this morning I travelled east one half mile then north one mile. Saw a ravine with plenty of dry wood and thick bushes. Here, making a bed of bushes, I slept until sundown. I then proceeded, travelled all night, wading through several branches of the Big Horn. This morning my moccasins were worthless and I threw them away.

"Feb. 12th: Today it snowed so that, not seeing the mountains, I was compelled to guess at the road. Stopped at midnight and slept in a snow drift.

"Feb. 13th: Crossed Piney Creek, struck the lake at 3 P.M. and now knowing where I was regained the road and arrived here at 8.30 P.M. very sore and completely exhausted.

I have the honor to be, lieutenant,
Your Ob't Serv't,
George Grant
Sergeant Co. E 18th U. S. Infantry."

Sergeant Grant's report is a masterpiece of the undramatic, the unemotional. When his horse gave out and his comrades deserted him he merely says, "I became separated from the others for the balance of the journey." He mentions wading streams and sleeping for two nights on the prairie without a fire, does not comment that this was in wet clothes in subfreezing temperature. He tells that his moccasins wore out and he threw them away, but does not add that he walked for two days in the snow shoeless. His last words—"very sore and completely exhausted"—are a classic understatement. Actually he never fully recovered. When his superior officers sent his report to Washington and asked if something could be done for him, they were told that no money was available but they might apply for a Medal of Honor for him. They did, and he got it.

Down on the Staked Plains in Texas five other messengers won Medals. General Nelson Miles with a force of infantry and cavalry came upon a large party of Kiowas and Comanches. The soldiers charged and drove them off. It was at this action that a Captain Chaffee gave his famous command.

"Forward," he cried. "If any man is killed I'll make him a corporal."

General Miles followed the Indians across the desert until water gave out, then returned and camped on the Sweetwater River. Food was running low. The wagon train had been cut off and captured by the Indians. Two scouts, Billy Dixon and Amos Chapman, with a sergeant and three troopers volunteered to go back to Camp Supply for rations.

They rode by night, hid by day. The second morning they saw a group of horsemen in the distance and thought it was the advance guard of a supply train. By the time they found out that it was a party of Kiowas it was too late to take cover before the Indians' first charge. The men dismounted and fought their way through the swirling mass of savages to a small knoll on top of which there was a shallow buffalo wallow. Only five of them made it, three wounded. One of the troopers, Smith, lay where he had fallen, apparently dead.

The men took turns digging frantically with their knives to deepen the wallow, and shooting to keep back the Indians. As the day wore on, more than one hundred Kiowas made repeated charges until the sides of the knoll bristled with arrows like a porcupine. The deadly fire of the troopers drove them back each time before they reached the top of the knoll.

It was a question of whether thirst would get them before their ammunition ran out. Their canteens were on their horses, dead on the plain. Two of the wounded men became delirious, maddened for water. Then a thunderstorm came up. As the rain pelted into their hole, the men dropped on their bellies and lapped it up, mixed with mud and their own blood.

Late in the afternoon, when they were down to their last few rounds of ammunition, the old scout and buffalo hunter, Amos Chapman, eyed Smith's body on the plain with its full cartridge belt.

"Keep the infernal savages off me, boys," he said. "I'm going after that belt."

He dashed down the knoll, ran to Smith and dropped to his knees. As he started to take the belt off, Smith moved. He was not dead. Later Chapman described what happened next.

"Did you ever try to shoulder a wounded man?" asked Chapman. "Smith was not a large man, but I declare he seemed to weigh a ton. Finally I laid down and got his chest on my back and his arms around my neck and got up with him. It was as much as I could do to stagger under him, for he could not help himself a bit. By the time I got twenty or thirty yards, about fifteen Indians came for me at full speed on their ponies. They all knew me and yelled 'Amos, Amos, we have got you now.' I pulled my pistol, but I couldn't hold Smith with one hand, so I let him drop. The boys in the buffalo wallow opened on the Indians just at the right time, and I opened on them with my pistol. There was a tumbling of ponies and scattering of Indians, and in a minute they were gone. I got Smith up again and made the best possible time, but before I could reach the wallow another gang came for me. I had only one or two shots in my pistol, so I didn't stop to fight but ran for it. When I was about twenty yards from the wallow, a little old scoundrel that I had fed fifty times rode almost on top of me and fired. I fell, with Smith on top of me, but I didn't feel any pain. I thought I had stepped in a hole. The Indians couldn't stay around there a minute, the boys kept it red hot. So I jumped up, picked up Smith, and got safe into the hole. 'Amos,' said Dixon, 'You are badly hurt.' 'No, I am not,' said I. 'Look at your leg,' said he. And sure enough the leg was shot off just above the ankle joint, and I had been walking on the bone, dragging my foot behind me. In my excitement I never knew it, nor have I had any pain in my leg to this day."

Old scouts and hunters were fond of telling tall tales. Smith was brought in under fire, but none of the rest of the party ever confirmed Chapman's story of how his foot was shot off.

Smith was almost dead, with a bullet through his lungs. Before he died he asked his comrades to prop him up in the wallow so that the Indians could see him and think that there was one more man to defend it.

When night fell, the Indians pulled off. At daylight Dixon set out, with only four cartridges, to try to get back to Miles. He met a detachment of cavalry and guided them back to the knoll. Smith was buried in the wallow that he had helped to defend in death, and the Medal-winning survivors were carried back to Camp Supply.

5

MEDALS AT A MASSACRE

"SOMEDAY I'LL CATCH YOU in the open. When I do, I'll cut your heart out and eat it."

The Sioux Chief Rain-in-the-Face said that. He said it to Captain Tom Custer. The Captain was officer of the day at an Army post where Rain-in-the-Face caused some minor trouble. He ordered the chief to be locked up in irons. When he got out, the Sioux vowed vengeance.

Tom Custer had won the Medal of Honor for two separate acts of valor during the Civil War by galloping into the enemy lines and capturing battle flags. Now he was a captain with the Seventh Cavalry on the frontier. His older brother, George Armstrong Custer, commanded the regiment.

Colonel Custer was a very colorful figure. He rode at the head of his troops in cream-colored buckskins, his long hair falling over a red bandanna around his neck, his four stag hounds capering around his horse. Some people loved him and thought he was the greatest of cavalry leaders. Some people hated him and thought he was vain and cruel—a witless "glory hunter." But everybody agreed that he was absolutely fearless.

He had graduated from West Point in 1861 at the foot of his class. Before the war was over he had risen to become a major general. After the war, when the Army was greatly reduced in size, officers who wanted to stay in the service had to step down in rank. Custer became a lieutenant colonel.

More words have probably been written about George Armstrong Custer than about any other American soldiers except Washington, Grant, and Lee, because he commanded in one of the most famous battles in American history. It was the Battle of the Little Big Horn, better known as the Custer Massacre or Custer's Last Stand. Twenty-four men won the Medal of Honor in this battle.

By a strange chance it was a peaceful action of Custer's in 1874 that set the stage for the Battle of the Little Big Horn in 1876. The government had made a treaty with the Sioux that gave the Indians much of South Dakota, Montana, and Wyoming. The treaty said that no white man would settle or hunt in this country, or even pass through without permission from the Indians.

Then the government broke the treaty by sending Custer and the Seventh Cavalry into the Black Hills country to make a survey. Custer found gold. When he reported it prospectors flocked into the area. No treaty could keep white men from gold.

The Sioux had a medicine man, Sitting Bull, who hated

white men. He had great influence with the young braves of the Sioux and the Northern Cheyenne. He advised them to leave the reservation. Thousands of them did. They gathered around Sitting Bull and retreated into the Bad Lands. The Army was sent after them.

They tried to surround the Indians with three columns of troops. The Seventh Cavalry was with the eastern column. The scouts found the trail of a large Indian village on the move. Custer's regiment was sent to follow it, with orders to wait for the rest of the column if he found that the trail led into the valley of the Little Big Horn River.

Custer was offered four troops of the Second Cavalry and three Gatling guns before he left the column. He refused them, saying that the Seventh could whip any number of Indians alone. That was his first mistake. He wanted all the glory of victory for his own regiment.

The trail did lead into the valley. Custer ignored his orders and followed it. That was his second mistake. He did not know how many Indians were in the valley. His Arickaree Indian scouts told him it was the biggest village they had ever seen. Custer did not believe them. That was his third mistake. Actually it was the largest gathering of Indians in history, probably over 15,000, with 2,500 to 3,000 fighting braves. Custer had about 600 men.

When he got in the valley, and before he had seen the Indian village, he divided his regiment. That was his fourth mistake.

He called Captain Benteen to him and said, "Take three troops and move to the left, pitch into anything you come across, and report to me."

He told Captain McDougall, "Take the pack train and one troop and follow Benteen."

That was his fifth mistake. Except for one hundred rounds in each trooper's cartridge belt and saddle bags, the mules of the train were carrying all the amunition.

Custer then moved into the valley about twelve miles. Here he said to Major Reno, second in command, "Cross the river with three troops and move forward as fast as you can. We will support you."

Reno's men formed for the charge on the other side of the river. They looked back. Custer had pulled the remaining five troops away from the river into the hills. He was sitting his horse on a bluff, his buckskins gleaming in the sun, waving his hat. That is the last anyone ever saw of George Armstrong Custer—alive.

As Reno's 112 men swept around a bend in the river and came in sight of the Indian village they gasped with astonishment. As far as the eye could see down the floor of the valley were Indian tepees. There was a horse herd of more than 20,000 ponies. And pouring out of the village toward them were thousands of mounted, screaming savages.

To charge into this mass would be madness. Reno dismounted two troops to form a battle line and sent his Indian scouts to hold the left flank. The Arickaree scouts promptly fled and were not seen again for days. The howling Sioux and Cheyenne braves swept behind Reno's force. He took shelter in a clump of woods, looking desperately behind him for the support that Custer had promised.

His ammunition already running low, Reno decided that the only way he could keep from being wiped out was to fight his way through the Indians, recross the river, and gain the crest of a hill where he could dig in and wait for Custer. He remounted his men and charged through the ring of redskins. He could not reach the ford by which he had crossed the river. He had to recross at a point where only one horseman at a time could scramble up the steep bank under a hail of bullets and a shower of arrows.

Reno's men would all have died at this crossing except that, suddenly, most of the Indians turned and thundered back down the valley. They were leaving to attack Custer, but Reno did not know this. He completed his crossing, formed his line, and gathered his dead and wounded.

Meanwhile Benteen, with his three troops and followed by the mule train with the desperately needed ammunition, was still looking for more Indians off to the left. He was about ten miles from the battle when Custer's bugler reached him with a note that said:

"Benteen, come on—big village—be quick—bring packs."

Benteen turned his men and galloped back. He reached the point where Reno's men were dug in, out of ammunition. Benteen's men shared their few cartridges, and all waited for the slow-moving mule train to come up. Even if they could find Custer, they would not be much help to him without ammunition.

But nobody knew where Custer was. The bugler who carried the note had left him on a hill almost four miles downstream and did not know what he was planning to do. When the ammunition came up, Reno and Benteen started to move in that direction. They heard distant rifle fire. Then it stopped. They assumed that Custer had been beaten off and was circling back to join them or to bring up the main column from the rear.

When the firing stopped, the thousands of savages came streaming back up the valley to renew the attack on Reno, forcing him back to his position on the hill. It was at this point that the first of his men won the Medal of Honor. A mule, still carrying the lifesaving ammunition, broke away from the train and galloped toward the Indian lines. Sergeant Richard Hanley took off in pursuit.

You can never figure out what a mule is going to do. Hanley had almost caught it when it swerved and galloped across in front of the Indian line. Hanley followed, the target for every Indian rifle. Again he almost caught the crazed animal. Then the mule skidded to a stop, wheeled around, and galloped back across the Indian front. Hanley would not give up that ammunition. He turned and followed the mule, bullets kicking dust around his horse's feet and his comrades shouting to him, pleading with him, to come back. Finally the stubborn beast stopped. Hanley grabbed the halter and lugged the mule back to his own lines. His mad race had lasted for twenty minutes, but none of the thousands of bullets and arrows that had been aimed at him at short range had found their mark.

For the rest of the day, Reno's men continued their dogged fight. The Indians got on a higher hill behind them. The troopers could not reach them with their carbines or revolvers. This was one time when the Indians were better armed than the soldiers. The troopers had single-shot breech-loading Springfield carbines. Many of the Indians had Henry repeating rifles. One sergeant had a Sharps buffalo rifle, a gun he had bought himself. A dead shot, he finally cleaned the Indians off the nearby hill and kept them off.

Night fell. A hideous night. The soldiers could hear the Indians but could not see them. Down in the valley the Indians held a scalp dance. Wild chants and the beating of tom-toms told the tired troopers that the redskins were working themselves up to renewed attacks at daybreak. And several times during the night, the white men were thrilled with hope when they heard the sound of a cavalry bugle which, they thought, was from the relief column. It was an Indian with a captured bugle playing the cavalry calls to torment them.

At dawn the Indians galloped out of the mist in a desperate charge to overrun the hilltop position. As they came up the slope more than 300 carbines spoke from the foxholes that the troopers had dug with their knives and spoons. Although they outnumbered the soldiers ten to one, the redskins could not gain the top of the hill.

As the day wore on, thirst started to take its toll. The river was only 150 yards away, but it seemed like certain death to cross those few yards in the face of the Indian fire. Finally some men could no longer endure the piteous cries of the wounded for water. Nineteen men volunteered to make the dangerous journey to get water for the wounded or die in the attempt.

They looked over the ground. The plain ran downhill, flat and without cover for about eighty yards. From this point to within fifty feet of the river was a gully which would give them some protection. On the other side of the river were bushes full of Indians.

The four best marksmen among the volunteers each

took three rifles. One by one they ran to the gully, crawled down it, and found what cover they could at the end nearest the river. Then in small groups the remaining fifteen water carriers made their dash for the gully, each with as many canteens as he could carry and with several large camp kettles.

When they were all sheltered in the gully they called to the sharpshooters, "All right. We're ready." The four men started to pick off Indians in the bushes across the river. The Indians replied with a hot fire at the marksmen. While they were trying to hit the sharpshooters, the water carriers ran to the river, only a few yards from the Indians on the other bank, scooped up water in the camp kettles, and dashed back to the gully. Bullets sang around them, several drilling holes in the camp kettles. But any Indians that rose out of the bushes to take careful aim were promptly knocked over by one of the marksmen.

Back in the gully the volunteers filled the canteens from the camp kettles, crawled up the gully, and dashed up the hill, under constant long-range fire from the Indians. They kept this up for four hours. Although several of the men were wounded, none, thanks to the sharpshooters, was killed. All nineteen men were awarded the Medal of Honor.

As the day drew to a close the Indians melted away from in front of the besieged troopers and set fire to the grass at the head of the valley. Through the smoke, the soldiers could dimly see teepees being taken down. The Indians were on the move. Their scouts had reported the approach of the main column of troops—the column that Custer was supposed to have waited for before entering the valley.

When the column, under General Terry, reached Reno's men, both commanders asked, "Where's Custer?"

Both answered, "I thought he was with you."

Next morning they found Custer—or what was left of him and the 223 men who were with him.

Nobody knows what happened at the Custer Massacre. There was no white man left to tell the tale. Later the Indians would not talk, or told wild, conflicting stories in an effort to avoid punishment. One story told by the Indians is that all Custer's men went crazy and shot each other.

Apparently Custer had planned to cross the river about four miles downstream from Reno's position and attack the lower end of the village. He never reached the river. He was caught in the open on the side of a hill. He must have been taken by surprise because he never had a chance to take a defensive position.

From the position of the bodies of the men and horses it looked as though three troops had dismounted and tried to form a line near the foot of the hill. The Indians apparently got their horses with most of the ammunition in the saddle bags, since there were only seventy dead horses on the battlefield. Some of the troopers died here. Others, when they ran out of ammunition, took cover in a ravine. Their bodies were found, sprawled on top of each other, at the bottom of the ravine where they had tumbled when the Indians shot the defenseless men from the sides.

Near the top of the hill was a ring of thirty dead horses that had obviously been shot by the soldiers to form a breastworks. Within this ring were the bodies of Custer and most of the officers.

A trooper who was assigned to help bury the dead wrote a description of the battlefield. He said:

"From what I saw of the field it appeared to me that there was very little time for Custer and his men to make any sort of defense. Most of the bodies were naked, which would indicate that as soon as the warriors had finished their bloody work, the squaws had time to rob the bodies of clothing and strip the horses of saddles. While doing this they mutilated the bodies. After being scalped the skulls were crushed in with stone hammers and the bodies cut and slashed. Many arrows had also been shot into the bodies—the eyes, neck, and stomach. I observed especially the body of Captain Tom Custer, which was the worst mutilated of all."

Tom Custer's heart had been cut out. Later Chief Rain-in-the-Face said that he had eaten "some of it."

It is not really true to say that there was no survivor of the Custer Massacre. There was one, and he earned a Medal of Honor—but they don't give Medals to horses.

Lieutenant Nowlan, who was with General Terry's column, hastened to the battlefield to look for the body of his friend Captain Keogh. Near the ravine a horse was standing. Nowlan approached. It was Comanche, the Captain's mount, his head drooping over the body of his dead master. For two days the animal had faithfully stood there, without water and wounded in eight places, waiting for his rider to mount.

Lieutenant Nowlan drew his revolver to put the animal out of his misery. He couldn't do it. Several troopers gathered around.

"Do you think we could save him?" asked one.

"Naw, he's too far gone," said another.

"We could try," said a third.

They gave the horse water and bathed his wounds. Slowly they led him for fifteen miles to the bank of the Big Horn River, where a padded stall had been built on a supply steamer. The steamer took him to a hospital. There he recovered.

The new colonel of the Seventh Cavalry issued an order. It said:

"The horse Comanche, being the only living survivor of the bloody tragedy of the Little Big Horn, shall to the end of his life be preserved to the utmost limit. He will not again be ridden by any person nor will he ever be put to any kind of work."

For sixteen years Comanche, saddled and bridled and led by a trooper, marched in every parade of the Seventh Cavalry. He lived to be twenty-eight years old, a ripe old age for a horse. When he died his body was mounted and given to the University of Kansas. In the museum of the university, the sole survivor of Custer's Massacre still proudly stands.

6

MEDALS FOR SABOTAGE

THE MARSHAL OF DODGE CITY was there, as was the Deputy Marshal of Cripple Creek and a group of Texas Rangers. The quarterback of the Harvard football team was there, as was the captain of the Columbia crew and Yale's champion tennis player. They were mixed in with some Cherokees, Chickasaws, Choctaws, and Creeks; with some buffalo hunters, prospectors, stagecoach drivers, professional gamblers, and four Baptist and Methodist ministers. But most of the men were plain cowboys—cowboys with strange names like Happy Jack of Arizona, Cherokee Bill, Smoky Moore the Bronco Buster, and Rattlesnake Pete.

They were milling around on a dock in Tampa, Florida, trying to get to the war. And the future President of the United States was running up and down the dock trying to get the ship to take them.

These were the Rough Riders, the most unusual regi-

ment in the American Army, or any other army. They were
called Teddy Roosevelt's Rough Riders, but actually the
future President was their lieutenant colonel. Their commander was Colonel Leonard Wood, one of the Medal-
winning "messenger boys" of the Indian wars. He won his
Medal by carrying dispatches one hundred miles in a single
day through hostile country, seventy miles mounted and
thirty miles on foot after his horse gave out.

Their proper name was the First United State Volunteer Cavalry, and most of them were from the frontier in
Arizona, New Mexico, and Oklahoma. Every man was an
expert with a horse and gun. They had fought desperadoes,
Indians, Mexicans, snakes, steers, and each other. Now
they were going to Cuba to fight Spaniards.

By 1898 Spain had lost most of her far-flung colonies in
the New World, which Columbus had discovered for her
back in 1492. First Mexico, then all the countries of South
America, had declared and won their independence. Spain
had nothing left except some islands in the West Indies—
principally Cuba and Puerto Rico.

Cuba had started a renewed fight for independence in
1895. The United States was sympathetic to the Cuban
battle for liberty, particularly after Spain sent a very cruel
general to suppress the rebellion. The farmers of Cuba
were feeding the rebels. The Spanish General decided to
put a stop to this by herding the farmers into the towns and
not letting them grow anything. This would starve out
the rebels. Of course, it would also starve everybody else,
but the Spanish General didn't care. To him, it didn't
matter if all Cubans starved.

It needed only a spark to bring the United States to the

aid of the Cubans. When the spark came, it was a big one. The United States battleship *Maine* had been sent to Cuba to protect Americans there. In the dead of night the quiet of the harbor of Havana was shattered by a deafening explosion. The vast hulk of the *Maine* was lifted from the water by an undersea blast. The ship burst into flames, broke apart, and 260 sailors and Marines died. It was thought, although never proved, that the vessel was torpedoed by the Spaniards. The cry "Remember the *Maine*" swept through the nation, and the United States declared war on Spain.

It was not a very big war. There were two naval battles. Admiral Dewey wiped out a Spanish fleet in the harbor of Manilla in the Philippines. Admiral Sampson wiped out another fleet at Santiago, in Cuba. On land there were several skirmishes and the twin battles of El Caney and San Juan.

It was at the charge up San Juan Hill that the Rough Riders won fame. Although they had been recruited because they were expert riders, their horses had been left behind in Tampa. They fought the entire war on foot. At San Juan they had to pass along narrow trails through a dense jungle to the base of the hill, under constant fire from unseen Spanish snipers in trees.

Behind the jungle snipers, Spanish regulars were well protected in trenches and blockhouses on the top of the hill. From where the jungle ended, the hillside was bare of cover. Mixed with other dismounted cavalry, flanked by infantry, and led by Teddy Roosevelt on a big horse, the wildly cheering Rough Riders stormed up the hill. Volley after volley from Spanish rifles and artillery tore gaps in their lines but failed to stop them. As they came on into the very muzzles of the guns, the Spanish panicked and fled.

There was a second line of defense, but a battery of Gatling guns was brought up to clear that out. Before dusk the Americans looked down the other side of the hill into Santiago. The main part of the war on land was over.

A man can be as big a hero in a little war as in a big one. Medals of Honor were won by 111 men in the war with Spain. On land, most of the Medals were for unusual valor in saving wounded comrades under fire. Sergeant Alexander Quinn, of the Thirteenth Infantry, was typical of the Medal winners.

The Thirteenth was supporting the dismounted cavalry. Early in the battle, Quinn's company was pinned down by Spanish fire. A lieutenant tried to go forward. He was dropped by a bullet. Quinn, a big bull of a man, dashed out and picked him up like a baby. As he returned to the line the lieutenant died in his arms.

Then a private named Wile, the best shot in the company, crept out about a hundred yards to a point where he could do deadly work as a sniper. Suddenly he threw up his hands and rolled over. A Spaniard in a palm tree had shot him through the lungs. Again Quinn dashed across the hundred yards of bullet-swept hillside and picked up the wounded soldier. Again the man died in his arms.

Later the same day Quinn saved a third wounded man, a major. As he was dressing the major's wound a shell burst overhead, wounding the major again and knocking the dressing out of Quinn's hand, but leaving him untouched.

The plight of the wounded was a desperate one in the Cuban jungle. A wounded man, alone in the jungle, would watch with dread as giant land crabs crawled around him on the jungle floor, waiting. He knew that if he lost consciousness, the powerful claws of the crawling crabs would soon be tearing at his flesh.

In the Navy, the most outstanding act of bravery was performed by eight American sailors who sank an American ship. Their leader, Lieutenant Richmond Hobson, was not supposed to be a fighting sailor. He was a "naval constructor"—a man of science and engineering who planned how to build ships.

Hobson had been working on a plan for an unsinkable mine sweeper to clear the mines out of Havana harbor. He took it to Admiral Sampson, commander of the Atlantic Squadron.

Sampson studied it, thought it was good. Then he said, "Right now I'm more interested in a sinkable than an unsinkable."

"I beg your pardon, sir?" said Hobson.

"I want to sink a ship—one of our own," continued Sampson. "We've located the Spanish fleet hiding in the harbor of Santiago. We can't get at them because of the forts at the mouth of the harbor, and I'm sure they won't come out to fight—we're much stronger than they are. I want to sink a ship to block the narrow channel in the harbor so that they can't sneak out past us at night."

"That should not be hard," said Hobson.

"It's not as easy as you think," replied the Admiral. "The ship will have to pass the fort and land batteries at point-blank range. It will be under fire from the Spanish

fleet. It has to be turned across the channel. If it doesn't
sink in exactly the right spot, it won't block the channel."

"What ship do you plan to use, sir?" asked Hobson.

"A collier, the *Merrimac.*"

The *Merrimac* was 330 feet long. It's not easy to make a
big ship sink like a stone. Hobson wrestled with the problem all that day and all that night. He pored over plans of
the ship, a chart of the channel, an almanac showing the
moon and tides. Next morning he returned to the Admiral.

"I've figured out two ways we could do this, sir," he said.
"We might cut the heads off the rivets holding six plates
in the side of the ship below the water line. We could
mount small cannon in the hold, pointing at the plates.
When we fire the cannon they will blow out the plates.
The ship will go to the bottom in less than three minutes."

"That seems like a good idea," said the Admiral.

"It is—except for one thing. This job should be done
just before daylight, when the moon is setting and the tide
is high. If we don't do it the day after tomorrow, we'll
have to wait a month. And it will take three days to cut
off those rivet heads."

"Well," said the Admiral, "what's your other plan?"

"Simply to mount seven long cans, each containing
eighty pounds of gunpowder, against the outside of the
ship twelve feet below the water line. They can be held in
place with ropes going under the keel. An electric primer
in each can, with wires running to the bridge, will fire
them when we're ready."

"How can the ship be turned in the narrow channel?"
asked the Admiral.

"We'll take the port anchor from the bow and rig it at

the stern on the starboard side. When we approach the spot we'll swing the bow toward the left of the channel and drop the starboard bow anchor. When it grabs, the stern will swing around across the channel, and we'll drop the stern anchor. They'll hold for the few minutes it takes the ship to hit bottom."

"And who is going to do this?" asked the Admiral.

"Why, I am, I hope, sir," replied Hobson. "And the fewer men the better. I'll need six men."

"And what's going to happen to you and the men?"

"The underwater explosion shouldn't hurt us. We'll tow a lifeboat, jump into it after we blow the torpedoes, and take our chances of drifting out with the tide."

"All right, you can try it," said the Admiral. "Good luck and may God be with you."

"There is just one more thing, sir," said Hobson.

"What's that?"

"May we take two warheads from Whithead torpedoes in the hold of the ship—to explode if anything goes wrong?"

"Absolutely not," cried the Admiral. "They'd blow you all to Kingdom Come. I won't permit you to commit suicide."

The plan was put in work. Gangs from several ships swarmed over the *Merrimac*, taking off her stores and hauling the heavy anchor chains from their wells and laying them along the deck. Coal passers shoveled the coal from the bunkers so that it would not hinder the rush of incoming water. Gunners prepared the powder cans and electric wires. Boatswains rigged the ropes to hold them. A battleship came alongside, lifted one of the 14,000-pound an-

chors from the bow with its heavy boom, and carried it to
the stern.

A signal was sent to the fleet for an electric generator—
an electric machine they called it then. There was not one
in the fleet. The charges would have to be set off by batteries, several batteries laying on the deck above each can.
This called for another man, as the cans would have to be
exploded individually.

Selecting the seven men was the biggest problem. More
than 600 men volunteered and fought for the honor of
this dangerous duty.

A fellow lieutenant approached Hobson and said, "Remember me, buddy, I was your roommate at Annapolis.
You can't leave me out."

A midshipman said, "You taught me ship construction,
sir. You have to take me so that I can show you how well I
learned."

An old chief boatswain said, "These gold stripes on my
arm mean twenty years without a misconduct charge. If
that doesn't rate a place in this crew, I don't know what
does."

The hardest man to turn down was the Captain of the
Merrimac. It was his ship; he was entitled to stay with her.
He went to the Admiral. Sadly the Admiral told him
that this was a job for an engineer, not for a line officer.
He did not tell him that it was a job for a young man—the
Captain was too old.

Hobson told his seven men their simple duties and rehearsed them over and over. It was planned that when the
ship got within range of enemy guns, all but the helmsman
would lay down at their posts. A cord from each man's

ankle would run to the bridge. When Hobson pulled the cord once, it meant get ready. Three pulls meant execute the job.

At one o'clock in the morning of June 3, 1898, the *Merrimac* started toward the entrance to the harbor of Santiago. A full moon shone down on the seven Spanish warships at anchor in the harbor. Grim Morro Castle, bristling with guns, loomed over the harbor entrance. Batteries of artillery lined the banks of the channel. There was not a light, not a sound, as the *Merrimac* steamed slowly ahead.

A relief crew handled the approach. Two miles from the entrance they left in a launch, still protesting that they wanted to go in with the ship. Only the seven men were left with Hobson. As the ship crept down the path of the moonlight on the water they held a last whispered rehearsal.

"Murphy, what's your duty?" asked Hobson.

"When you pull the cord three times I cut the bow anchor away with an axe. Then I fire can number one," replied Murphy.

"Charette, what's yours?"

"I handle the engine room telegraph. When the engines stop, I go to can number two and fire it. Then I run to can number three and fire that."

"Deignan?"

"When I get the order I throw the wheel hard aport, lash it, and run to fire can number four."

"Clausen?"

"I stand by number five and fire it when four goes off."

"Kelly and Phillips?"

"We stop the engines on signal, open the sea cocks, then run to cans six and seven. I fire six and Kelly fires seven," said Phillips.

"Montague?"

"I stand by the stern anchor with an axe and cut it away when the stern swings across the channel."

"Right," said Hobson. "And after each man does his job he is to run to the stern and lay down under the taffrail until I join you."

The silent *Merrimac* crept on. The shape of the black castle grew clear in the moonlight. The Spaniards must see them soon. Two thousand yards from the entrance Hobson started his dash.

"Full speed ahead," he ordered.

The water creamed around the bow of the collier as she gathered speed.

"Steady astarboard."

"Astarboard she is, sir," repeated Deignan.

A thousand yards. Five hundred yards. Still silence from the dark castle. Then a gun flash from near the water's edge. A picket boat had spotted them. As if on signal, the fort and the Spanish batteries opened up. Shells screamed overhead, burst against the sides of the ship. Still the tough collier went on. It was in the channel now. Three ship lengths—two—and it would be at the narrowest point.

"A touch of port helm," said Hobson.

"A touch of port, sir," repeated Deignan.

"You may stop the engines, Charette."

"The engines are stopped, sir. May I go to my station?"

The ship coasted the last few feet, shells bursting around

her like a display of fireworks. Above the din Hobson shouted, "Hard aport!"

"Hard aport, sir," replied Deignan.

The vessel coasted straight ahead.

"Hard aport, I said!" cried Hobson.

"The helm is hard aport and lashed, sir."

The rudder had been shot away. The ship would not steer. It was coasting straight ahead toward the anchored Spanish fleet, which had already opened fire on it with every gun.

Hobson gave Murphy's signal cord three strong jerks. There was still a chance that the vessel would sheer across the channel when the bow anchor took hold.

The first powder can went off with a bang. Murphy had done his job promptly and well. Then there was silence except for the bursting shells. Hobson shouted, "Fire all charges!"

Charette came running along the deck. "Cans two and three will not fire, sir. The batteries have been hit. They're shattered all over the deck."

"Try all the others!" cried Hobson.

Only can number five went off. The batteries or wires to the others had been broken by gunfire.

The ship continued to coast gently toward the end of the channel. She had too much headway for the bow anchor to hold. Then, with a grating noise, the bow struck a sunken reef. The stern started to slowly swing around. If the stern anchor was dropped at just the right moment the channel might still be blocked. Hobson ran aft. As he reached the taffrail he found Montague crouched under it, axe in hand.

"Cut away the anchor," cried Hobson.

"It's gone, sir," said Montague. "A shell cut the lashing and broke the chain."

As he spoke, the bow slipped off the reef and the slowly sinking ship continued to drift toward the Spanish fleet in the wide part of the bay.

The men huddled flat on the deck as the collier shuddered and the din of bursting shells increased. Rifle bullets from the nearby bank were pinging off the sides with a noise like a shooting gallery. Shell fragments clanged on the deck around them, but nobody was hit.

A dark figure on hands and knees crept toward them. They were being boarded. Hobson raised his revolver. Murphy knocked his arm up just in time. It was Kelly from the engine room. He had been knocked out for a few minutes when a shell exploded near him.

For eight minutes, ten minutes, the men hugged the deck behind the doubtful protection of the rail. The deck slanted forward. The ship was sinking by the bow. Then she heeled over sharply to starboard.

Charette cried, "She is going to turn over on us, sir."

"No," replied Hobson. "She'll right herself in sinking."

The ship lowered its head like a tired horse. The shell fire ceased. The ship plunged forward, and a wave of water rushed up the deck, pinning the men to the rail. Then the deck dropped from under them, and they were dragged down in a whirlpool of swirling water.

They came to the surface and looked for the lifeboat. It was gone—sunk or cut away by shell fire. Nearby a catamaran floated—a raft like a small diving float, buoyed up by empty cans, that was carried aboard warships for survivors to cling to if the ship sank. It was tied to the sunken mast. The men swam to it and held on.

Spanish small boats rowed toward them with lanterns, looking for survivors. They ducked all but their noses under water. The boats passed. Some of the men wanted to cut the catamaran loose. Hobson forbade it; the tide would carry them farther up the bay.

Dawn broke. The men were shivering and gasping with cold, getting weaker. They could not hang on much longer. Someone spoke.

"A steam launch is coming toward us, sir."

It was a large launch, a captain's gig. Hobson made a quick decision. He hailed it.

"Is there an officer on board to accept the surrender of a group of American sailors?"

A squad of Spanish Marines ran to the bow and leveled their rifles. An order rang out in Spanish. The Marines lowered their guns. Hobson swam to the launch. A bearded officer helped him aboard. Hobson was surprised to find himself facing Admiral Cervera, commander of the Spanish fleet. The Admiral said one word in Spanish— *"Valiente."* He had to admire the valiant men who had tried to bottle up his fleet.

The Americans were treated well as prisoners. After a few weeks they were exchanged and returned to the States as heroes. The *Merrimac* did not block the channel, but as it turned out, Admiral Sampson was wrong when he thought that the Spaniards would not come out to fight.

Admiral Cervera was a brave and proud sailor. When Santiago fell, he brought his fleet out to face the much stronger American squadron. Every Spanish ship was sunk.

Many of the officers became American prisoners, and Hobson was able to repay the kindnesses they had shown him when he was their prisoner. On the Navy side at least, it was a gallant and courteous war.

7

MEDALS IN CHINA

IN CHINESE their name was I HoChunan. That means "Fists of Righteous Harmony." That's what they called themselves. Because the word "fist" was in their name, everybody else called them Boxers. When they set out to kill all the white men and native Christians in China, it was called the Boxer Rebellion.

Their cause was partly religious, partly patriotic. Missionaries from Europe and America had converted thousands of Chinese to Christianity. The Buddhist priests of China did not like this. Several foreign countries had grabbed large sections of China and were seeking to get more. The Chinese Emperor did not like this.

In 1899 there had been a great drought in China. The crops withered in the field. Millions of people were starving. The Boxers convinced the ignorant people that this was the fault of the "foreign devils." Thousands of peas-

73

ants flocked to the red Boxer banners. The priests published messages that they said were from the Buddhist Gods:

SACRED EDICT

From the Lord of Wealth and Happiness.

The Catholic and Protestant religions are insolent to the Gods. They enrage heaven and earth. The rain clouds no longer visit us. Eight million spirit soldiers will descend from heaven and sweep the empire clear of all foreigners. Then will the gentle showers once more water our land.

The Boxers did not wait for the spirit soldiers. They started to slaughter missionaries and Chinese Christians in outlying districts, killing them with the "death of a thousand cuts." Many who escaped made their way to Peking, the Chinese capital, to take refuge in the legations of their countries. When the Boxers started to menace the foreign legations, the ambassadors wired to their governments for help.

Four hundred and twenty Marines and sailors came to Peking from ships on the coast. Fifty-seven of them were Americans. The rest were British, French, German, Austrian, Italian, Russian, and Japanese. These few men held off tens of thousands of Boxers and, toward the end, the Chinese Imperial Army in a two-month siege that is one of the most famous in history. Twenty-one of the Americans won the Medal of Honor.

The British legation in Peking, with its five acres of land, was the best suited for defense. All the civilians were brought there. A Chinese prince had a large estate next to the legation. The Marines took it over and quartered 2,000 Chinese Christians in it. Night and day, men and women, white and Chinese, worked to build barricades around the area. Women cut up their dresses, curtains, sheets, tablecloths, and sewed them into bags. Chinese Christians dug up the Prince's lawns, filled the bags with dirt. Marines and sailors built them into breastworks.

Every day the Boxers gathered outside the barricades. Yellow-robed Buddhist priests chanted prayers to excite them. The fanatics charged the barricades in waves, armed with large swords and thirty-foot, iron-tipped bamboo spears. As the screaming mob came within range, the Marines mowed them down with rifle and machine-gun fire.

Those that escaped the deadly fire ran back to the priests and said, "You told us that the bullets of the foreign devils could not harm us. Look at all who are dead."

"We said that if you had faith the bullets of the foreigners could not hurt you," replied the priests. "Do you have faith?"

"Yes," said the survivors.

"Have you been hurt?"

"No," replied the survivors.

"That proves what we say is true. Those that were killed were not as good as you. They did not have enough faith. Go back and charge again."

The ignorant peasants returned to the attack again and again until they learned, the hard way when bullets hit them, that the priests were lying to them.

Meanwhile more warships had arrived at the coastal city of Tientsin, ninety miles away. A relief column of 2,000 men started for Peking by train. Thirty miles up the line the tracks were torn up. They repaired them and went on to the next break in the rails. Day after day they repaired the railroad ahead of them and fought off hordes of Boxers until they came to a destroyed bridge that could not be repaired. They had to turn back.

While they were gone, the fleet on the coast had no word from them. The telegraph had been cut, and no messenger could get through the swarms of Boxers. A week passed, ten days, two weeks. The worried captains of the foreign ships decided to sail up the Pei Ho River to land reinforcements. They called upon the Chinese forts at the mouth of the river to surrender. The Chinese refused and opened fire on the fleet when it tried to pass. The fleet landed Marines and captured the forts. This brought the Chinese Army into the fight on the side of the Boxers.

In Peking it seemed as though the well-armed Marines could hold out against the spears and swords of the Boxers until their food or ammunition gave out. Food was rationed. The foreigners were eating the mules and horses that they had brought inside the barricades. The Chinese Christians were eating their dogs. But when the Chinese Army, with rifles and artillery, joined the Boxers it put a different face on the siege.

It was at this point that several of the American Marines won their Medals. There was a thirty-foot wall around Peking. Inside this, around the section of the city that contained the Emperor's court, was another wall sixty feet high and forty feet wide, called the Tarter Wall. Part of the Tarter Wall overlooked the legation area. The Chinese Army held this wall and could pour down rifle and artillery fire from its top into the legation defenses. They had to be driven off.

There were ramps to the top of the wall near the American and German legations. Taking the Chinese by surprise, the Marines of both nations charged up the ramps, wiped out the Chinese between the two ramps with rifle fire and bayonets, then turned, back to back, and cleared the Chinese from the section of the wall overlooking the legations. While they lay on the top of the wall, holding the Chinese back with rifle fire, Christian Chinese coolies trotted up the ramps behind them with sandbags to build barricades.

The Chinese, too, built breastworks of sandbags some distance down the wall, but they could not shoot into the legations from this point. Then they tried a clever trick. They started to build a wall of large bricks in front of their own barricade by pushing the bricks out one at a time from the end of their breastworks and crawling behind those already in place to lay more. This wall slanted toward the American barricade, and when it got high enough, the Chinese could shoot down into the American position.

A few British Marines and Russian sailors came to join the Americans and Germans in a desperate effort to take the Chinese defenses. Captain Myers, of the United States Marines, called the officers together.

He said, "We will attack at two o'clock in the morning. When the Chinese hear us coming in the dark they will concentrate their fire on the middle of the road on the top of the wall—they always do. But we won't be there. We'll be running down both edges of the wall in single file.

We'll go over their new brick wall at both ends. If the rest of you fellows will mop up between the brick wall and the sandbag breastworks, we Americans will go around the sandbags and get behind them."

As the hour of attack approached, the allied Marines quietly pulled bags out of their breastworks so that they could get around the ends. On a signal from Myers they started running down the edges of the wall. The Chinese behaved just as Myers expected. They poured a heavy fire down the middle of the Tarter Wall. Not a man was hit. Before they knew what was happening, Americans, British, Germans, and Russians had swarmed over both ends of the wall and were among them with the bayonet.

The Americans kept going—went around the end of the sandbag barricade. They drove off the men who were defending the breastworks and got among the reserves before many of them woke up. Some were sleeping in little shacks of matting that they had built on top of the wall. The Marines kicked out the sticks that held up the shacks. The Chinese woke up when the roof fell in, and as they struggled to get out, Marines plunged their bayonets through the thin matting.

There were fifty men in the attacking force. A Chinese colonel was killed, and brigade and regimental headquarters flags were captured, indicating that the Chinese must have had at least 5,000 men in the area—odds of one hundred to one. Of course, many of the Chinese were sleeping.

Most of the Medals given to the defenders of Peking were given for "gallantry in action," not for any one brave act but for bravery beyond the call of duty day after day, every day for two months. One American who can be singled out for a specific act of bravery is Navy Gunner's Mate John Mitchell.

Mitchell found the barrel of a Chinese cannon, more than one hundred years old, in a cellar of the Prince's palace where the Chinese Christians were staying. He hauled it out and cleaned it up. He took the wheels and axle off a water cart and got a piece of timber and some wire.

His mates watched him, asked him what he thought he was doing.

"I'm building a piece of field artillery. It may come in handy," replied Mitchell.

The French Marines looked at each other, shrugged their shoulders. *"Il est fou,"* said one.

Some German Marines strolled over to where Mitchell was working. *"Er ist verrückt,"* they said.

The Japanese were too polite to say it out loud, but they whispered to each other, *"Bakamono da."*

In any language that means "He's cazy." Everybody was sure that Mitchell's homemade cannon would blow up in his face the first time he fired it.

Mitchell kept on, cheerfully working to mount his gun. When he finished it he borrowed some powder from the Germans, some shells that would fit the gun from the Russians, and some fuses from the Japanese. He christened it the Old International, loaded it, and wheeled the old cannon to the breastworks. Everybody moved back to a respectful distance and waited to pick up the pieces when the gun exploded. It didn't explode. It blew the side out of a building where the Boxers were rallying for another charge.

Mitchell and Old International soon became the heroes of the legation. When the Boxers were seen massing in front of the British or American breastworks the call went out, "Bring the gun."

The bursting shells terrified the Boxers. They ran off to make their assault elsewhere. From the other end of the barricades came the cry, *"Apportez le canon,"* and Mitchell went tearing off to help the French.

He attached ropes to his cannon and got some coolies to pull it. Every day he was seen racing through the streets from point to point in the defenses to answer the cry *"Bring die kanone"* from the Germans or *"taiho wo motte koi"* from the Japanese.

Everybody wanted the gun when they were hard-pressed, but nobody else would ever fire it. They were still sure it would explode the next time it went off. Mitchell gave out before the gun did when he was badly wounded during the last days of the siege. Before he fell, the brave gunner's mate and his century-old build-it-yourself cannon probably saved the legation and everybody in it.

While the gallant defenders of Peking were holding off the Boxer hordes, ships were steaming under forced draft from the corners of the earth to bring help. American ships brought the Ninth and Fourteenth Infantry from the Philippines under General Chaffee—the Indian-fighting Captain who had said, "If any man is killed I'll make him a corporal." British ships brought the Bengal Lancers and a regiment of Sikhs from India. Russian ships landed infantry and mounted Cossacks. Japan, the closest country, sent the most men.

The Boxer fighting in Peking had started early in June.

It was mid-August before a force was built up at the coast that was considered strong enough to attempt to relieve the besieged city. They had to march ninety miles inland, fighting their way through hundreds of thousands of Boxers and a Chinese Army that outnumbered the 20,000 allied troops by at least ten to one. The Chinese Army was defeated in two pitched battles near the coast and retreated to the walls of Peking to defend the city.

The Boxers continued to attack the column as it advanced. The advance guard of the allied force would come upon a waiting crowd of 1,500 or more men and boys armed with spears, swords, pitchforks, and clubs. While the Boxers roused themselves to a frenzy of excitement by chanting *"Sha—sha"* (kill—kill), the little advance guard would deploy and mount a machine gun. When the screaming fanatics charged, the advance guard would begin shooting and keep it up until there were no Chinese left to shoot. Then the column would march on.

Worse than the Boxers and the Chinese Army was the heat. In the Chinese summer the broiling sun turned the rain-starved land into a plain of ankle-deep, choking dust. In a letter to his family, one soldier said:

"The heat is torture. I saw men fall down unconscious from it. I saw men who had gone crazy, and I saw men die from it. Last night a man who was crazed jumped into the river and tried to kill himself."

Men who dropped in the ranks could not be left behind to suffer the death of a thousand cuts at the hands of the Boxers. Progress was slow as they were carried forward, or while the column waited for them to recover.

The Chinese in Peking, well armed with modern rifles

and artillery and greatly outnumbering the attackers, felt safe behind their thirty-foot wall. When the relief column reached the city the officers held a council of war. It would do no good to lay siege to the place—the Christians in the legation would starve before the Chinese in the city. Besides, word had reached them that other Chinese armies were marching to the defense of the city. They had to attack.

It was decided that the Japanese would go around to the left side of the city. The Russians would attack the main gate at the front, with the Americans on their right flank. The British and troops of other nations would go around to the right side of the city. The attack was to be made at eight o'clock in the morning, but the Russians, wanting to get credit for being first in the city, jumped the gun and attacked too soon. They forced the gate but were driven out again with fearful loss.

The Americans were facing a blank wall across a moat swept by heavy artillery fire from towers on the wall. They could not stay where they were. They either had to retreat or cross the moat. One by one the men of two companies of the Fourteenth Infantry dashed across the moat and plastered themselves against the base of the wall, where the Chinese artillery could not reach them. Here they seemed to be pinned down. There was no gate through the wall, and they had no equipment with which to scale it. One of the thirty-nine men of the relief column who won the Medal performed his brave act here.

His name was Calvin Titus. He was not a fighting soldier. He was a musician, a member of the band. As the two companies hugged the wall he crawled over to his captain.

"Sir," said Titus, "I think I can climb that wall."

"How?" said the Captain.

"I'm a pretty good climber," said Titus. "I could climb anything when I was a kid. This wall is made of very old bricks, and the ends of a lot of them are broken. I think I can get holds for my fingers and toes on the broken bricks. I can take up a rope so that the rest of the men can follow me."

"Go ahead and try it, boy," said the Captain. "We'll be right behind you."

Titus examined the wall, found a likely place to begin. Slowly he started up, the rope slung over his shoulder. His comrades held their breaths as he advanced a few feet, paused to look for new holds, then inched upward. As the human fly crawled higher over their heads a few soldiers started after him, while others stepped back to pick off any Chinese who might lean over the top of the wall to fire down at the climbers.

Titus expected to have to fight his way over the top. His act was no less brave because he did not know, while he was climbing, that the Chinese above him had run down the wall to help beat off another Russian attack on the gate. Before the Chinese returned, Titus and his few followers had reached the top, and the rest of the two companies were swarming up the ropes. The American flag was the first on the wall.

The Americans quickly drove the Chinese from their positions at the top of the gate, and the Russians and the rest of the Americans rushed through. But the Americans were not the first to relieve the legation. That honor fell to the British.

When the English and Indian troops went around to the right side of the city, a few Chinese Christians sneaked out of the legation area and opened a gate for them. The British went through unopposed. Then one of the Chinese showed them the bed of an old, dry canal which led into the legation area through an underground sluice gate.

The people in the besieged legation were first alarmed, then overjoyed, to see the bearded, turbaned, grinning Sikhs come running out of the canal bed to join the weary defenders at the barricades. The siege of Peking was over.

It is interesting that all but one of the seven nations that fought side by side with the Americans in China have, at some time, been "the enemy" in a war with the United States—England, Germany, Japan, Italy, Austria, and France. (Yes, America did fight France in a little naval war that lasted from 1797 to 1800.) The only one of the allies that the United States has not fought against is Russia.

8

MEDALS FOR MACHINE GUNS

THE ARCHDUKE FRANCIS FERDINAND sat proudly erect in the back seat of the open car, returning a dignified salute to an occasional cheer from the crowd. Beside him his pretty, blonde wife, the Duchess of Hohenberg, bowed and smiled, trying to conceal her nervousness.

The Duchess had cause to be nervous. That morning she had narrowly escaped death when her husband neatly fielded a bomb which had been thrown at the car and knocked it to the street before it exploded. Now they were on their way to the hospital to see two of the Archduke's aides who had been hurt by the explosion.

The crowd that lined the path of the car was silent and sullen. Most of these people in the city of Sarajevo were Serbians. Austria-Hungary had annexed their part of Serbia in 1908. Now it was June 28, 1914, and the Serbs still had no love for Archduke Ferdinand, heir to the Austrian throne.

As the car slowed to turn into Franz Joseph Street, Gavrillo Prinzep pushed forward in the crowd. He loosened the revolver in his belt. Prinzep was a student—possibly not a very good student, for newspaper accounts say that he was only in the eighth grade although he was eighteen or nineteen years old. But he was a good Serbian patriot. Although he had nothing against the Archduke personally, Prinzep thought that by killing him he might attract the attention of the world to the unfair way that Austria-Hungary was treating Serbia.

Prinzep took three quick steps toward the slowly moving car, drew his revolver, jumped on the running board, and started to blaze away. His first shot struck the Duchess in the stomach; another hit her in the neck. A third smashed into the Duke's throat. The Duchess fell forward across her husband's knees. The Duke tried to speak. Bright blood splashed from his mouth across his scarlet tunic and the brilliant sash and medals on his chest.

The Archduke and his wife were the first of nearly eight million people who were to die in the war that followed Prinzep's act. Some call it the European War—that's where the fighting took place. Others call it the World War, as it was, finally, with twenty-eight nations involved, including such remote lands as Siam and China, Liberia and Costa Rica.

What followed the murder of the Archduke was like the story of the old woman and the pig: "The dog began to chase the cat, the cat began to kill the rat, the rat began to gnaw the rope"—and so on as one act led to another.

Austria declared war on Serbia.

Russia mobilized her army to help Serbia.

Germany declared war on Russia.

France had a treaty to support Russia and declared war on Germany.

Germany invaded neutral Belgium to attack France.

Great Britain had a treaty with Belgium and declared war on Germany.

Turkey came in on the side of the Central Powers—Germany and Austria.

Italy came in on the side of the allies—France, England, Russia, and others.

For three years America stayed out. Principles that went back to Thomas Jefferson said that what happened in Europe did not concern the United States. But the ruthless way Germany was fighting shocked many Americans. They did not like the invasion of helpless little Belgium. They were horrified at the sinking by a German submarine of the British passenger liner *Lusitania*—an act that drowned over 1,100 innocent civilians, 188 of them Americans.

Then in 1917 Germany went too far by announcing that she was going to torpedo all ships, including American ships, bound for Allied ports. At the same time, American secret agents got a copy of a note that Germany sent to Mexico proposing that Mexico join Germany if the United States entered the war. For this, Mexico was to receive the states of Texas, New Mexico, and Arizona when the United States was defeated.

On April 2, 1917, President Woodrow Wilson asked Congress to declare war on Germany to "make the world safe for Democracy." During the next nineteen months, 123 Americans won the Medal of Honor.

By the time America entered the war, there had been a

revolution in Russia. The new Russian government, fore-
runner of the present Communists, had made a separate
peace with Germany. Italy and Austria were fighting what
amounted to a private war around the head of the Adriatic
Sea. The main fighting was in France, where the English
and French were bogged down in the mud, facing the Germans in a double line of trenches that stretched for 300
miles from the shore of the North Sea to the border of
neutral Switzerland.

In three years a new pattern of trench warfare had developed. Each trench was a long slit in the earth seven or
eight feet deep, with a parapet of sandbags facing the
enemy trench. From a firing step behind the sandbags
sentries watched the enemy through periscopes. In front
of each trench were rows of tangled barbed wire strung on
posts. Between the barbed wire was No Man's Land, an
area of shell holes and endless, ever-present mud.

The battle front moved slowly back and forth as one
side or the other attacked at different points on the line.
The attack started with a barrage from massed artillery
designed to flatten the enemy's barbed wire and prevent
him from bringing up reinforcements to the threatened
point. Then the barrage lifted, and the infantry went
"over the top" of the sandbags, ran across No Man's Land,
jumped into the enemy trench, and went to work with the
bayonet.

New weapons came into play. The Germans used poison
gas—mustard gas that burned, phosgene gas that choked,
tear gas that blinded. They first released this from gas
tanks in the front-line trenches when the wind was right
to blow it toward the Allied lines, but gave this up after a

few unhappy experiences in which the wind shifted and blew the gas back on the Germans. Then both sides switched to poison-gas artillery shells. To counter this, the gas mask was developed, and troops went into action looking like men from outer space.

The idea for another new weapon came from a British colonel who, before the war, had visited a fair in Belgium where there was a display of American farm equipment. He saw a caterpillar tractor in action, its endless metal treads carrying the machine through ditches and over rocks on the uneven ground. Years later, as the Colonel looked out over the muddy, shell-pocked No Man's Land, where a wheeled vehicle could not travel, he remembered the tractor.

He thought that a tractor with a gun protected by sheet armor could go through the shell holes, knock down the barbed wire, and crawl right into the enemy trench, spitting death as it went.

Plans were drawn. England started to build what they called land cruisers. It was all very secret. The new weapon was to be an unpleasant surprise for the Germans. It was so secret that nobody was allowed to use the words "land cruiser." The people who were rolling the armor plate were told that the material was for water tanks or fuel tanks. The word "tank" became the code word for the weapon. And that's what it's still called.

But the important weapon was not the tank or poison gas. It was the machine gun. Machine guns were not new. They went back to the American Civil War. But they had never been a major weapon. In the World War both sides used tens of thousands of them. They were usually set up in and behind the front-line trenches, where they could blanket No Man's Land with their deadly fire. Each gun was in a machine-gun "nest"—a hole in the ground surrounded by a parapet of sandbags.

Artillery was not very effective against machine-gun nests. When a barrage was on, the machine gunners ducked down behind the sandbags and were protected from anything but a direct hit. When the barrage lifted, the gunners raised their heads and mowed down the advancing infantry. Before they could advance beyond the front lines the infantry had to silence the machine guns. Most American Medal winners won their awards knocking out machine-gun nests.

The various ways of knocking out a machine-gun nest—if you had the Medal of Honor type of courage—are indicated by the citations of some of the Marines who won the Medal. This is the only war in which Marines were awarded the Army, as well as the Navy, Medal of Honor.

The award to Sergeant Louis Cukela says: "Disregarding the warnings of his comrades he crawled out from the flank in the face of heavy fire and worked his way to the rear of the enemy position. Rushing a machine-gun emplacement, he killed or drove off the crew with his bayonet, bombed out the remaining part of the strong point with German hand grenades and captured two machine guns and four men."

Private Joseph Kelly "ran through our own barrage a hundred yards in advance of the front line and attacked an enemy machine-gun nest, killing the gunner with a grenade, shooting another member of the crew with his pistol, and returning through the barrage with eight prisoners."

The citation does not say what method Corporal John Pruitt used. It merely says that he "single handed, attacked two machine guns, captured them and killed two of the crew. He then captured forty prisoners in a dugout nearby."

Army Lieutenant Samuel Woodfell used several weapons to win his Medal. He started out with three men, who were shot down by a machine gun. Woodfell picked up a rifle and shot three of the machine-gun crew. There was an officer left in the machine-gun nest, and the rifle was empty. Using it as a club, the Lieutenant swung at the officer and missed. He then jumped into the hole and started to wrestle the officer in the mud. As they grabbed at each other's throats, Woodfell was able to get out his pistol and shoot the German.

Wiping the mud out of his eyes, the Lieutenant crawled to a second machine-gun nest and emptied his pistol into the crew, killing all three of them. Now his pistol was empty, too, and there was another machine gun. Woodfell snatched a pickaxe from the ground, jumped into the third nest, and beat the brains out of the German gunners to capture his third gun.

There was one man who set a record for capturing machine guns that will never be equaled. If there is one Medal of Honor winner who can be called the all-time champion of champions it is Corporal Alvin York.

When America entered the war Alvin York was teaching Sunday school and leading the church choir in a little town called Pall Mall in the mountains of Tennessee. He wanted to keep it that way. He did not know what the war was about and he did not want to know. Deeply religious, he felt that all war was wrong and he wanted no part of it.

York had been born in a log cabin in the mountains. Here there was no school in the winter. It was too cold for children to sit in the unheated building or to wade the unbridged streams on the way to it. York had gone to school for a few weeks in the summer, where he had learned to read well enough to study the Bible and to write well enough to keep a war diary that told a great story of mental anguish and calm courage.

This was Daniel Boone and Davy Crockett country, on the edge of "the Dark and Bloody Ground." York's great-great-grandfather hunted 'coon with Davy Crockett, and on a beech tree near York's birthplace Daniel Boone had carved:

> D. BOON
> cillED A BAR
> in   thE
> YEAR 1760

York had been brought up on stories of Boone and Crockett—stories like the one about how Daniel Boone shot squirrels so as not to muss them up. He didn't hit the squirrel; he missed it so close that the rush of air from the passing bullet knocked it dead. Such stories may not all have been true, but they inspired every mountain boy to be a crack shot with the long rifle. Also there were no supermarkets in the mountains. If there was meat on the table it came from the woods or from a turkey shoot.

York was a champion turkey shooter. He described it like this:

"A bunch of us would get together with our hog rifles. We called them hog rifles 'cause we used them to hunt wild hogs in the woods. They was handmade muzzle-loading guns about six feet long, and they weighed about twenty pounds. You loaded them with loose black powder, a greased patch of cloth, and then a round lead bullet. You pushed all this down tight with a ramrod. Up to a hundred yards we liked 'em better than any modern rifle.

"A fellow that had a turkey would bring it around and sell shots of it for ten cents apiece. You could buy as many shots as you had dimes if you wanted to. Then we'd lay a log on the ground and tie the turkey's foot to a stake behind the log so that only his head showed above the log when he was standing up straight. Then we measured off sixty yards and took turns shootin' at the turkey's head. We shot off hand—that is, standing up without a rest. The first fellow that busted the turkey's head got the turkey.

"Of course the turkey didn't stand still for all this. Sometimes he'd wave his head around and sometimes he'd keep it down most of the time and just stick it up for a minute. You had to be fast. I was usually pretty lucky. We ate a lot of turkey at our house."

In the summer of 1917 York's turkey-shooting, Bible-reading, hymn-singing life was rudely interrupted by a little red card that he received in the mail. Uncle Sam wanted him in the Army. York did not want to go. He had nothing against Germans, and he firmly believed that it was wrong for any man to kill another man. It said so in the Bible. And the Bible couldn't be wrong.

When York registered for the draft he wrote on the

paper, "I don't want to fight." Then he went to his minister. The minister told him that because their church thought that all war was wrong, York might be excused from the draft. He wrote to the local draft board, the state draft board, even to President Wilson. It was no use. York had to go.

Alvin York went to training camp, the first time he had ever been out of the mountains. He made up his mind to do everything he was told to do—except kill Germans. He was a model soldier, obeyed every order. Once he almost rebelled when he was told to police up the barracks area by picking up cigarette butts. This did not seem fair to York— he did not smoke.

After a few weeks of this, York went to his captain and told him how he felt about war and killing. He asked if he could be given some duty which would not compel him to kill.

Captain Danforth listened patiently and then said, "York, I've heard a lot of stories like this. Mostly I think the men who tell them are just plain cowards, but I don't think you are. I think that you're sincere. Let me talk to the Major about it."

A few days later Captain Danforth took York to see Major Buxton. The Major started the conversation by saying, "While we're in this room we're not a major and a captain and a private. We're three Americans trying to figure out something that's hard to understand. Now, York, tell me—why don't you want to fight for your country?"

" 'Cause my church teaches that war is wrong," said York.

"Is that part of your church's creed?"

"We don't have no creed. We just believe the Bible, and the Bible says, 'Thou shalt not kill.' "

"Do you accept every word in the Bible just as you accept the Sixth Commandment?"

"I do," said York.

"Well, how about when Jesus said, 'He that hath no sword let him sell his cloak and buy one'? That's in the Bible, too."

York admitted that was in the Bible. "But," he said, "Jesus also said, 'If a man smite you on one cheek, turn the other to him.' Killing Germans ain't turning the other cheek."

"Do you suppose," said the Major, "that the Christ who chased the money changers out of the temple with a whip would stand by and watch the Germans drive the helpless Belgians from their homes without helping them?"

The argument went on far into the night. The Major was from Providence, Rhode Island, and was the first Yankee whom York had ever met. He was amazed that the Major knew the Bible as well as he did. For every quotation that York could give against war, the Major had one that seemed to endorse fighting for the right. He explained that York had a duty to God and a duty to his country, and that Christ had said, "Render unto Caesar that which is Caesar's," meaning that Christians should serve their country when they were called.

York was more confused than ever. He asked for some time to think it over. A few days later he again approached Captain Danforth.

"Captain," he said, "Will you tell me again what this war is about?"

The Captain took a deep breath. "The Major told you what the Germans did to the Belgians. We are simply going over there to put a stop to that sort of thing. We are going to make peace."

"Captain," said York, "I could think a lot better in the mountains. May I have a pass to go home for a few days?"

York got his pass. He returned to the mountains. He greeted his mother and visited his minister. Then he climbed a mountain and knelt in the woods on its top to pray. He prayed all evening, far into the night, asking the Lord for help. Suddenly, he heard in his mind the words of the Captain: "We are going to make peace." He remembered the words of Jesus on the Mount: "Blessed are the peacemakers." Now the way was clear. The Lord had told him what to do. He walked down the mountain—a six-foot, redheaded, two hundred and ten pounds of bone and muscle peacemaker. Alvin York went off to fight.

In the north of France, near the Belgian border, lies the Argonne Forest. The Germans had captured it at the beginning of the war and fortified it with strong trench systems, four deep. It was hilly, rocky country, cut by deep ravines and covered with dense underbrush. Behind it ran a railroad line that was the principal supply route of the German Armies. It was a tough place for an attack, but if the Allies could capture the railroad it might mean the collapse of the whole German front.

On the night of September 25, 1918, over a million Americans quietly moved in to relieve the French in front of the Argonne to start the biggest and last important battle of the war. One of them was Alvin York.

For the first few days of the fight, York's division was in reserve. The American advance swept forward and easily took the first two lines of trenches. Then progress slowed. The reserve was called up. On October 8, York went into action.

His company started out across a valley at six in the morning. From a hill on the other side machine-gun fire mowed down the first wave. The survivors dropped to the ground. The guns were carefully hidden so that no one could tell where the fire was coming from. York's platoon sergeant, Harry Parsons, crawled along the line and told three squads to follow him in an effort to get behind the guns.

The Sergeant, three corporals, including York, and thirteen privates crawled off to the left and wormed their way around the hill. Here dense underbrush hid them from the Germans. In single file they kept going—in York's words they "sorter flitted from bush to bush, like Indian fighting." It was quiet now; the guns were well behind them. There were no Germans in sight. The Americans started to work their way back toward the hill.

They came to a path, followed it. As they rounded a bend they almost ran into two German stretcher bearers. The Germans fled. Chasing them, the Americans came to a small clearing on the bank of a stream. Around a little shack in the clearing were fifteen or twenty Germans. This was the headquarters of the machine-gun battalion on the hill. A German major, two lieutenants, and several orderlies and runners were eating breakfast, their weapons laid aside. When the Americans opened fire the Germans immediately surrendered.

At the sound of the firing behind them, the Germans on the hill swung their guns around. As the Americans started to line up their prisoners, a blast of machine-gun fire from the hill swept the clearing, killing six and wounding three of the Americans. The rest hit the dirt. Some huddled close to the prisoners for protection; others rolled behind trees.

York was caught out in the open, about twenty-five yards from the nearest machine gun. More guns were turned around, and thousands of bullets clipped the brush and kicked up dust around him. York fired at the head of the German manning the nearest machine gun, hit him between the eyes.

A second German put his eye to the sight of the machine gun. York fired again. He picked off every German who raised his head to sight a gun. The head of a German is a lot bigger than the head of a turkey. At this distance York could not miss. When it was over he said he thought that he had fired about twenty-five times. There were twenty-four dead Germans.

In desperation, a German officer and five men charged down the hill with fixed bayonets. They had only twenty-five yards to run. Some of them would surely get through. York's rifle was empty. He dropped it, stood up, drew his .45 automatic, and started to knock over the charging Germans—first the sixth, then the fifth, then the fourth, and so on. The first in line—the last to be shot—fell at his feet. He explained that this was the way they shot wild turkeys at home, getting the back one first so that the front ones wouldn't know what was going on and would keep coming.

At this point the major who had been captured with the headquarters company rolled over to York and yelled, "If you'll stop shooting I'll make them surrender."

"Go ahead," said York. "But try any tricks, and I'll blow your head off."

The major blew his whistle and called out in German. Slowly the men rose from behind the machine guns, their hands in the air. A few at first and then more and more came down the hill. When they stopped coming, York had eighty or ninety prisoners.

The problem now was what to do with them. They were well behind the German lines, with many more machine-gun nests between their position and the American front. York lined the prisoners up by twos, put his seven men along the line to guard them, and had the prisoners at the rear carry the American wounded. With the German major leading, York behind him with a pistol in his back, and a German lieutenant on each side, the little parade started over the hill straight through the German lines.

As they advanced, more machine guns swung around to fire. Each time they approached one, York poked the major in the back with his pistol and said, "Tell them to surrender."

The major blew his whistle and called out a command. Well-trained German soldiers did not disobey a major. They dutifully put up their hands and joined the parade. All except one. He reached for a grenade. As York said, "I had to tech him off."

The slowly lengthening procession marched through

the German line and into an American artillery barrage falling between the lines. York ordered double time through the bursting shells. He was a humane man. He was responsible for the prisoners. He did not want them to get hurt.

York had one more problem that day. When he got to the American battalion headquarters nobody would take his prisoners—there were too many of them. They told him to take them to regimental headquarters. Here he was told to take them to division headquarters. Finally, after a long march, he found a brigadier general.

"Well, York," said the general, "I hear you captured the whole German Army."

"No, sir," said York, "I only have one hundred and thirty-two."

When they mopped up the hill they found thirty-five deserted German machine guns.

9

MEDALS IN THE AIR

THE LITTLE BIPLANE SWOOPED DOWN into a small clearing beside the ground crew of a French observation balloon. The American pilot cut his engine, pushed up his goggles, and leaned over the side of the cockpit.

"Hey, you Frenchies," he called. "Come here."

The French soldiers started toward the plane, then grinned with delight as they recognized the flier.

"Ah, *c'est* Monsieur Luke," they cried. *"Qu'est que c'est,* Monsieur?"

"You see those two German sausages hanging over there?" said Frank Luke.

"Oui"

"Well, watch 'em. At six fifty-seven I'm going to shoot down the one on the left. At six fifty-nine I'll get the one on the right. Then I'm coming back here for you to sign a slip saying that you saw me do it, so that I'll get credit for it."

"*Mais certainment,* Monsieur Luke. *Bonne chance.*"

Luke gunned his engine and rose out of the clearing, dragging his tail through the top of a tree. There were no paved runways then. Any reasonably smooth field was an airport.

The Frenchmen strained their eyes through the gathering dusk. They could hardly make out the German observation balloons—Drachen—swinging lazily at the ends of cables two miles behind the enemy lines. They glanced from the horizon to their watches. Had it been anybody other than Frank Luke who made such a boast they would not have bothered to watch. But they had learned that Luke usually did what he said he was going to do.

At exactly 6.57 a burst of flame lit up the distant sky. Drachen number one was a mass of flaming hydrogen. The eyes of the watchers shifted to the right. At 6.59 there was another puff of flame on the horizon. The Balloon Buster had done it again.

Frank Luke was one of the two American airmen to win the Medal of Honor in World War One. The other Medal winner, Eddie Rickenbacker, would never have done such a thing. He would have shot down the balloons, but would have done it quietly, without boasting.

It is hard to imagine two men who were more dissimilar than America's two greatest fliers. Luke was twenty years old. Rick was twenty-eight—fairly old for a World War One pilot. Luke talked big and loud. Rick spoke softly, with a smile. Luke was disliked by most of his flying mates. They called him the Arizona Boaster. Rickenbacker was admired and respected by everybody.

The heroes had two things in common. Both were

superb fliers and both were absolutely fearless. But Luke's daring was foolhardy and reckless. Rick's was coolly and carefully planned. Luke paid no attention to orders and would accept no discipline. After going off alone on a balloon-smashing mission when he should have been flying in formation with his squadron, he frequently would not bother to come home at night or report in. He would stay with a balloon outfit—the balloon boys loved him—and go hunting again at dawn.

When Luke did not return from his last hunt his commanding officer said, "When he comes back I don't know whether I'm going to court-martial him and then recommend him for the Medal of Honor or whether I'll recommend him for the Medal first and then court-martial him."

Few fighter pilots took kindly to army discipline. Most of them were young, many in their late teens. They lived a gay, exciting life—and a short one. They thought that "eat, drink, and be merry, for tomorrow we die" was a reasonable motto—as it was for many of them. The average active life of a fighter pilot at the front was less than six weeks. Also, until General "Billy" Mitchell took command of the American air service, the pilots had great contempt for commanding officers.

Most senior officers had never been in an airplane, did not understand them, and did not trust them or the young idiots who flew them. They did not see what noisy planes could do in a war except frighten cavalry horses. Pilots called these nonflying commanders kiwies because, they said, a kiwi is a bird that cannot fly. They said that a kiwi's favorite type of plane was a flat-topped desk and that the only thing he loved more than his mother was the ground. When the colonels and generals were out of earshot, the pilots sang the kiwi song.

> Oh, we don't have to fight like the infantry,
> Shoot like the artillery,
> Ride like the cavalry.
> And we don't have to fly over Germany
> For we are the Ki-wee-wee.

When the war started, the military man's lack of faith in planes was understandable. It was only eleven years since Wilbur and Orville Wright had lifted the first plane from the ground. Although each Army had a few planes in its Signal Corps, they were new and untried experiments.

In the beginning, even the pilots did not think of fighting with airplanes. Planes carried no guns. They were to see with, not to fight with. When a French pilot saw a German plane in the air he might fly close to it, wave gaily, and call, *"Bon jour, mon ami."* The German would wave back, shout, *"Wiegehts,"* and each would fly on over the enemy trenches to see what was going on behind the lines. A few pilots took up rifles to take pot shots at their opponents, but this was not considered sporting. Flying was dangerous enough without shooting, too.

This did not last long. The Germans figured how to mount a gun on the nose of a plane, shooting through the blades of the propeller. The gun fired each time the propeller turned, so that the bullets went between the blades without shooting them off. The French and British quickly copied the gun. The war in the air was on.

But the main job of the airplane was not fighting. It was

observation—flying far behind the enemy lines to take pictures of what the enemy was doing. The single-seater fighting planes were to protect the slower, two-man observation planes from enemy fighters and to knock enemy observers out of the air.

By the time America got in the war, foreign generals had learned that planes gave a new dimension to warfare. But America had not learned. When the country went to war it had no fighters, only fifty-five slow training planes.

American pilots fought in castoff French planes. They were biplanes, called Nieuports, which had a wooden frame braced with piano wire and covered with cloth. The Nieuports had one bad fault. In a steep dive—frequently the best way to elude an enemy—the wings sometimes came off. Or, more frequently, the fabric ripped off and left the pilot with a wooden skeleton.

Although America did not have planes, it did have pilots who could fly rings around the new German Fokker fighters in the old French crocks. Because he fought longer, the all-time ace of aces (an ace was a pilot who had downed five enemy planes) was a German, Baron Manfred von Richtofen. He fought for nineteen months before he was killed and bagged eighty planes, an average of about four a month. Eddie Rickenbacker was in action about three months and had twenty-five confirmed kills, an average of about eight a month. Frank Luke's fighting career lasted only seventeen days, during which he knocked down eighteen Germans, better than one a day.

Fourteen of Luke's kills were observation balloons. Most pilots steered clear of balloons. Attacking them was suicide. They hung in the air at an altitude of from 200 to 2,000 feet, seemingly an easy target. But that target was surrounded by massed antiaircraft and machine guns on the ground, which threw a curtain of bullets, bursting shells, and "flaming onions" around it. And usually there was a formation of German fighters hanging high above the balloons, waiting to pounce on any low-flying planes that attacked them.

When Frank Luke first joined his squadron, fresh from the open spaces of Arizona, he looked at a Fokker far overhead and loudly asked, "Why do you fellows let that guy fly around up there? It's going to be different from now on. They won't do that with me around."

That was his greeting to his more experienced comrades.

A few days later he came back from patrol, jumped from his plane, and shouted to the other pilots.

"I got a Hun. He started to dive on me from above. I saw him coming and sideslipped, made a tight outside loop, and got on his tail. I let him have it right in the back. He started to spin, and I followed him down till he crashed."

The other pilots looked at him silently. Finally, one of them spoke: "Did anybody see you do it?"

"No, I guess not," said Luke.

There was another pause. "What's the matter?" continued Luke. "Don't you guys believe me?"

All except one of the other pilots silently turned and walked away. The exception was a young pilot named Joe Wehner. For some reason that nobody ever understood, Wehner attached himself to Luke like a faithful dog. They were as different as night and day. Luke was so slight in build that he did not look strong enough to fly a plane. Joe was a big hulk, a crack athlete. Luke was always bragging, long and loud. Wehner seldom spoke. The difference between the two young men is shown in the report that each made on his first confirmed kill.

Combat report—Sept. 12th 1918

"Lt. Frank Luke reports:—

Saw three Fokkers and gave chase until they disappeared toward Metz. Saw enemy balloon at Marieville. Destroyed it after three passes at it, each within a few yards of the balloon. The third pass was made when the balloon was very near the ground. Both guns jammed so pulled off to one side. Fixed left gun and turned about to make one final effort to burn it but saw that it had already started to burn. The next instant it burst into flames and fell on its truck, destroying it. There was a good field near our balloons so landed for confirmation. Attached is confirmation signed by Lt. Fox and Lt. Smith."

Luke was taking no chances that they would not believe him this time. Joe Wehner's report contained only eleven words.

"At 3,000 meters shot down Fokker south of Fismes. Visibility good."

When Luke started on his solitary balloon-busting hunts, Wehner flew after him to protect his friend. Luke's usual method of attacking a balloon was to get high above it, cut his engine, and dive silently down, hoping to catch the balloon crew and the antiaircraft gunners by surprise. If his first burst did not fire the Drachen, he made a fast skidding turn at tree-top level and zoomed up under the sausage for a second try.

Meanwhile Wehner hung far above. When the hovering Fokkers that were protecting the balloons started down for Luke, Joe dived into their formation, breaking it up, and taking on the five or six planes in combat to give Luke a chance to finish his job and get away.

While Luke was building his reputation as a balloon buster, Wehner was quietly piling up a score of Fokkers. Night after night both planes returned riddled with bullet holes, both fliers miraculously unhurt. Then came a night when Joe Wehner did not return.

The Americans were planning a big surprise push against the German line near a town called Conflans. They needed to mass troops and artillery at this point. But it would not be a surprise unless they could get rid of three German balloons that were watching the area. Luke was sent out to do the job. He was followed, as usual, by Wehner.

As Luke crossed the Meuse River near Verdun he saw five Fokkers in the distance. He looked up and back. Joe wiggled his wings to show that he had seen them too. Luke paid no more attention to the Fokkers. He swung far behind the German lines to come at the balloons from a surprise direction. He cut his engine and started down.

He lined his sights up on the big black cross on the side of the balloon. The German antiaircraft fire opened up. Machine-gun bullets ripped scores of holes in the plane. Shells burst around it in clouds of black smoke, rocking the ship in the air. "Flaming onions" threw showers of fire toward the fragile wings. Luke went on, recklessly ignoring the hail of fire. When the bag loomed before him a hundred feet away he sent a stream of incendiary bullets into the gas bag. With a mighty "swoosh" the hydrogen exploded. Luke stood his plane on one wing as he turned to escape the flaming gas and flew through the curtain of fire on the other side.

As he started toward the second balloon, Joe Wehner's plane flashed past him. Joe leaned out and fired a red flare —the danger signal. In the flaming sky, Luke did not see it. He kept on to down the second balloon. Wehner had broken up the formation of Fokkers, downing one. But now, unknown to Luke, a second group of seven German planes was above them.

When Luke ignored his danger signal, Joe turned to face the seven Germans. It was suicide to attack them from below, but it was death for Luke if the Fokkers got on his tail at that low altitude, where he had no room to maneuver.

Luke zoomed past the wreck of his second balloon, turned his head in time to see Joe's plane hurtling toward the ground, a mass of flames.

Luke went crazy as he watched his only friend burn. He hurled his plane at the Fokkers without even trying to maneuver. Approaching head-on, he shot the first one out of the air. Viciously he kicked his plane around and darted toward the side of the second one, his guns pouring a stream of lead into its cockpit. He turned again, but the Germans had had enough of this madman. They were streaking for home.

Almost out of gas, Luke started for the American lines. Ahead of him he saw four French planes circling around a two-seated observation plane, being held off by the tail gunner. Luke swept through the French, zoomed up under the belly of the German two-seater, and killed both pilot and observer with one quick burst.

In less than ten minutes Luke had downed two balloons and three planes—a feat that has never been equaled.

With the death of his only friend in the squadron, Frank Luke changed. Now his fellow pilots would have liked to be friends. A man like Luke was entitled to brag. But Luke no longer bragged. He no longer spoke. For the eleven days that remained of his life he was silent, reserved. He spent most of his time away from the squadron, living with the French, hunting balloons from dawn to dark.

On the night of September 29, 1918, just at dusk, a lone plane swooped down and circled an American balloon. The pilot leaned out and dropped something, zoomed up and away. The ground crew picked it up. It was a note. "Watch out for those three nearest balloons—Luke."

They watched the three sausages floating in the distance. Suddenly there was a burst of flame. Before it had died out there was another, and a third. Then darkness and silence. They excitedly phoned Luke's squadron headquarters to report the triple kill. That was when Luke's commanding officer could not decide whether to court-martial him or give him a medal.

He did not have to make that decision. Luke never came back. For a few days his headquarters did not worry. He was probably with the French. A week passed. They phoned throughout the area. No Luke. They waited for a report from the Red Cross that he was wounded or a prisoner. There was no report.

After the war was over, the Army set up a Grave Registration Service to find the unmarked graves of American dead. An officer of this service heard about an unknown pilot who had been buried in a little town named Marvaux. He went there to investigate and returned with an affidavit signed by fifteen of the townspeople.

AFFIDAVIT

The undersigned certify to having seen on the evening of Sept. 29th, 1918, an American aviator, followed by an escadrille of Germans, descend suddenly toward earth and then straighten out close to the ground where he found a German balloon which he burned.

He then flew toward Milly where he found another balloon which he also burned in spite of heavy fire which was directed toward his machine. There he was apparently wounded. He came on to Marvaux, where with his machine gun he killed six German soldiers on the ground and wounded others. He then landed his plane.

He got out of his machine and started toward a stream. He had gone fifty yards when he saw the Germans coming toward him. He still had strength to draw his revolver and defend himself, but a moment after he fell dead from a wound in his chest.

They dug up the body. It was Frank Luke. Without Wehner above him he had died far behind the German lines, fighting till his last breath.

When the Wright brothers made their flight at Kitty Hawk, Frank Luke was five years old. Thirteen-year-old Eddie Rickenbacker was starting to build his first automobile engine in his cellar. Fifteen years later, when America entered the war, Rick was one of the country's top racing drivers. He went to France as the chauffeur of America's commanding general, "Black Jack" Pershing.

Chauffeuring a general was tame work for a crack race driver. Rick wangled a job as instructor of mechanics at a French flying field, so that he could learn to fly. In an earlier effort to join the air service he had been turned down because he was not a college graduate. He had left school at fourteen to help support his mother after his father died.

Rick's flying was largely self-taught. Later, he described it like this:

"I remember when I thought it was time to try a tail spin. I knew what I was supposed to do. I knew you put the stick over and crossed the controls, but I had never seen anybody do it. I went up to about 12,000 feet and flew around for every bit of thirty minutes trying to get up my nerve to try the trick but I was too scared to begin. At last I said to myself, 'What's the matter with you? You've got to do this'—and I threw over the stick. She went into the spin all right, but I had her back to neutral after just one whirl, and I tell you I was glad when she righted."

Rick practiced every maneuver that a fighting plane could make and invented some of his own. His background as a race driver gave him two great advantages—an unerring judgment of timing and distance and a "feel" for his engine which told him just what it was capable of. Rick became a part of his plane. Together they were a deadly fighting machine.

Fighting in the air was a matter of maneuvers timed to a split second. When two fighters met, each jockeyed to get on the other's unprotected tail, throwing their frail crafts around in the air in a series of loops, barrel rolls, sideslips, and spins to avoid the opponent's spitting nose gun. Rick did this so well that he brought down more Germans than any other American, yet often returned without a single bullet hole in his own plane.

He was a scientific murderer, yet he wasn't a killer. This sounds strange, but Rick wasn't fighting men. He was fighting machines. To him, aerial combat was a contest involving engines and guns and the principles of aerodynamics. The man who employed these things most skillfully won the contest. The other man died.

Rick schooled himself to leave nothing to chance if he could help it. On one of his early patrols he was watching a plane below him that he was going to attack. Suddenly a machine gun stuttered into life behind him, and a row of holes was drilled in his wings. His only hope was a power dive. As his Nieuport screamed toward the earth the fabric ripped off his upper wings and fluttered out behind him. By masterful flying he nursed his ship home.

Stepping from the plane he said to his mechanic, "After you replace the fabric on the upper wing, put patches on the bullet holes in the lower wings. Paint a black cross on each patch. I want those to remind me, every time I step in the plane, not to go into a fight without first making darn sure of what's behind me."

Many pilots lost their lives because their machine guns jammed. This happened over and over again, principally because the ammunition was not uniform in size. After it happened once to Rick, he decided to load his own ammunition belts at night, carefully inspecting each cartridge and discarding those that might give trouble. Jammed guns were one risk that could be avoided by being careful. Rick avoided it.

Most of Rick's kills were made after he had been promoted to squadron commander, an assignment that many men considered a desk job. Rick did not. He got somebody else to do the paper work while he trained pilots, trained mechanics, and led two flights a day to patrol the lines to protect American observation planes and knock down German observers. Before breakfast and after dinner he went up alone looking for a fight—a coolly calculated, carefully planned, skillfully executed fight from which he always came out the winner.

The reckless, foolhardy, flaming career of Frank Luke was gallant and thrilling and vastly heroic. Flinging himself into the jaws of death without regard for the consequences was certainly "beyond the call of duty." But it was Rickenbacker who brought down the most planes. Equally fearless, Rick added skill and judgment to valor and lived to serve his country in another World War.

10

MEDALS FOR SACRIFICE

IN CHICAGO, the Bears were playing the Cardinals. In Washington, the Redskins were playing the Eagles. In Pittsburg, 2,500 pacifists had gathered in Soldiers and Sailors Memorial Hall to hear a United States senator call President Franklin Roosevelt a warmonger.

Almost everywhere the weather was good. Many people had taken the children downtown to see the Christmas decorations in the store windows. In the far West, late churchgoers were listening to sermons. In the Midwest, most people were sitting down to a big Sunday dinner. In the East, people were napping on the couch after dinner, reading the funnies to the kids, listening to the radio.

In New York, those who were tuned to N.B.C. were hearing Sammy Kaye and his Swing and Sway. Sammy had just read a poem entitled "When We're Apart"—a prophetic title for millions of Americans who would be apart for

four long years. Then, at 2.29 P.M. on this Sunday afternoon of December 7, 1941, an announcer broke in on the
program.

Stunned, startled, breathless, he said, "From the N.B.C.
newsroom in New York. President Roosevelt said in a
statement today that the Japanese have attacked the Pearl
Harbor in Hawaii from the air. I'll repeat . . ."

Just that. There was no declaration of war—that came
later. Out of the blue Hawaiian sky Jap planes suddenly
appeared to catch the Pacific fleet napping in the harbor
and to destroy the air force on the ground at Hickam Field.
In less than two hours America's great naval base in the
Pacific was knocked out of action. Eight of the nine battleships in the fleet were destroyed or crippled. Almost 3,000
Americans were killed.

America went to war with Japan and, on the other side
of the world, with Germany and Italy. In Europe, war had
been raging for two years—a war that had been creeping
up on America as German submarines sank American
ships. The German Nazis, under mad, fanatical Adolph
Hitler, had conquered Czechoslovakia, Poland, Belgium,
Holland, Denmark, Norway, France. The English were
dug in on their little island behind the wall of the Royal
Navy, under the umbrella of the Royal Air Force. The
German blitzkrieg (lightning war) had pushed far into
Russia, where the Communists were staging a last-ditch
fight at Stalingrad.

America was at war on a global front that stretched from
Australia to Siberia, a war in which 429 Americans were
to win the Medal of Honor.

America's reaction to the news of Pearl Harbor was one

of stunned, shocked, horrified surprise. The immediate comment, almost everywhere, was "Why, the dirty, yellow ———." Frequently, the next comment was "Those poor, stupid little Japs." Many people had listened to self-styled Far Eastern experts who gave the impression that the Japanese Navy consisted of two bathtubs and that most Japanese pilots were so cross-eyed they couldn't hit Lake Michigan with a bomb. It shouldn't take long to beat them.

They were very, very wrong. In the days that followed Pearl Harbor the news became steadily worse. Except for tiny Midway Island, every American outpost in the Pacific fell to the Japs—including the Philippines. The British lost Hong Kong. The Dutch lost all their bases in the East Indies. The Japanese fleet reigned supreme in the great ocean. The few American troops who were not killed or captured were forced "down under" to Australia.

In the Civil War, many Medals were given for capturing flags. In fighting Indians, they were given for carrying messages. In the Spanish-American War, for saving wounded comrades. In World War One, for capturing machine guns. There was no such pattern in World War Two. In the many types of fighting on a global front, with the variety of weapons used, no one kind of brave deed stood out. If there was a common denominator to the Medal awards in World War Two it was the number of Medals that were awarded to men who deliberately sacrificed their lives for their cause or their comrades. Of the fifteen Navy Medals given for acts of valor at Pearl Harbor, eleven were awarded to men who were killed performing their brave deeds.

There was Machinist's Mate Robert Scott. His battle station on the battleship *California* was at an air compressor below decks which provided jets of air to eject the spent shells from the 5″ guns above. An aerial torpedo crashed into the side of the *California* and blew a jagged hole in the side of the compartment where Scott was working. As water and oil flooded the compartment the other men of the detail left—but not Scott. He said, "This is my station. I'll stay here and give them air as long as the guns are going."

The watertight door of the compartment was slammed on the water that was flooding into the ship—and on Robert Scott. The air kept coming to the guns until the water drowned the compressor—and the man who served it.

Also on the *California* was Radio Electrician Thomas Reeves, a warrant officer. When the ammunition hoists stopped running, he formed a detail to carry shells by hand through a burning passageway. One by one the members of the party dropped from the heat and fumes. Reeves dragged them out and went back again and again for another shell. When only Reeves was left and he fell, there was nobody to drag him out. He died there.

The battleship *Oklahoma* was hit by four torpedoes in the first wave of the attack. She immediately started to capsize, with most of her crew trapped below decks. When she was later raised, 400 dead bodies were still in the ship. A few men who did not die owe their lives to Medal-winners Ensign Francis Flaherty and Seaman James Ward.

Flaherty was in command of a 14″ gun turret. It went under water when the ship capsized. When the crew forced the door open, the incoming water compressed the air in the turret, leaving a temporary breathing space. Ward

volunteered to help Flaherty get the other men out. Together they held flashlights and guided one man after
another to the submerged door, so that they could dive
out and swim to the surface. Flaherty and Ward were the
only ones who did not get out. The water rose around them
while they were helping the others and before they had
a chance to dive.

Chief Boatswain Joseph Hill swam back from safety to
die at his station. The battleship *Nevada* was the only
capital ship to get under way during the attack. Her skipper
tried to get her out of the harbor so that she could
maneuver to avoid bombs and torpedoes. There was no
crew to cast off the lines on the pier to which she was
moored. Hill led a party ashore to cast off. The bow of the
ship started to swing away from the pier with the tide.
Hill leaped into the water, swam to the ship, and climbed
aboard.

Going down the channel the *Nevada* was again attacked.
Her commander realized that she was sinking, would block
the narrow channel, and prevent other ships from escaping.
He swung his ship out of the channel, beached her, and
gave orders to let go the bow anchor. It was stuck. Hill
ran forward to attempt to free it. A brace of bombs brack-
eted the ship and blew Hill to his death.

There were so many acts of valor at Pearl Harbor that,
it would seem, it was almost necessary to die to win a
Medal. Chief Water Tender Peter Tomich, of the *Utah*,
won the Medal and died. Fireman John Vaessen of the
same ship was equally heroic, but was not awarded a Medal
of Honor.

The *Utah* was an old battleship that had been decom-

missioned and was being used as a target for aerial bombing. Because her deck was covered with flat layers of tim-
bers, the Japs thought that she was the aircraft carrier
Saratoga. They attacked her so viciously that she lasted
only eleven minutes after the attack began. Then she
started to turn turtle.

The order was given to abandon ship. To keep the lights
going so that men would not be trapped below in darkness,
Fireman Vaessen stayed at his post in the dynamo room.
Chief Tomich stayed at his post in the fire room to see that
all boilers were shut down to prevent an explosion. Tomich
went down with his ship. Vaessen was lucky.

When some of the crew of the *Utah* reached shore they
took shelter in a slit trench. Here, between bomb bursts,
they heard someone knocking on the hull of the capsized
ship. It was Vaessen. As the water had come into the
dynamo room he had made his way through a manhole
into the very bottom of the ship, where he huddled in an
air pocket, tapping on the steel bottom with a wrench.

Two warrant officers left the slit trench, found a small
boat, went back to the *Utah,* and answered his tapping.
Then they made their way through bursting bombs and
a hail of machine-gun bullets from strafing planes to get
a cutting tool from another ship. While the attack blazed
around them, they calmly cut a hole in the bottom of the
Utah and let Vaessen out.

During the first days of the war there was only one
bright spot in the news. Wake Island. For two weeks after
it was attacked on December 8, 1941, Wake held out
against everything that the Japs threw at it. It held out
with "the help of God and a few Marines."

Wake is a tiny atoll in the far Pacific, built by coral atop the crater of an underwater volcano. It is really three islands—Wake, Wilkes, and Peale—spread in a horseshoe shape around a lagoon. For years it was a bird sanctuary, inhabited only by tens of thousands of Japanese lovebirds, fluttering canaries, thieving pirate birds, and gooney birds. When humans did come to Wake, these gooneys made life miserable for them. Incredibly stupid, they would sit on runways and let planes run over them, or fly up into whirling propellers, knocking them out of alignment. They flew into aerials and antennae, broke the windshields of planes, and they kept air spotters on the alert by flying in perfect formation with motionless wings, looking like a V of distant planes.

Until 1935 the only thing to share the island with the birds were the Wake Island rats—gigantic, long-haired rodents with a great span of whiskers. Marines came to hate these rats worse than they hated Japs. The sound of bursting bombs made the rats frantic with fear and they fought the Marines for the dubious safety of foxholes. One fear-crazed rat leaped into a foxhole during an attack and sank his teeth firmly in a Marine's nose. He could not pull it off, and it hung there while he beat it to death.

In 1935 Pan American Airways built a small hotel on Wake and made it a stop on the trans-Pacific island-hopping route of their flying boats. In 1941 the government started to build a military installation. When the war started, there were 400 Marines, 1,200 civilian construction workers, and a few Pan-Am people on the island. And there were some newcomers—a dozen Marine pilots, among

them Captain Henry Talmage Elrod, the only man in the
Wake defense force to be awarded the Medal of Honor.

The Marine flyers had been hustled aboard the carrier
Enterprise at Pearl Harbor for a secret destination and
introduced to a new fighting plane—the Grumman Wildcat. Day and night the Navy flyers aboard briefed them on
this most recent combat plane. Then on December 3,
the Marines took off from the deck of the carrier to take
their station on Wake. The *Enterprise* turned and steamed
toward Midway Island.

It was Monday, December 8, on Wake when it was
Sunday, December 7, at Pearl—the international date line
was between the two. At about 7.00 A.M. that morning
Major James Devereux, commander of Wake's Marines,
walked out of his quarters with a radiogram in his hand.

He said to a brother officer, "I've just had this message
that the Japs attacked Pearl Harbor this morning. Of
course, it may be another false alarm. If it's verified, I'll
let everybody know."

It was verified. The Marines took their battle stations
on the low, sandy atoll. Hank Elrod led four of the Wildcats aloft on patrol. The rest were hurriedly armed with
100-pound bombs and then dispersed on the ground to
wait their turn on patrol. The Marines scattered to man
the island's six 5″ naval guns, twelve 3″ antiaircraft guns,
eighteen heavy and thirty light machine guns.

At 8.00 A.M. the bugle sounded "Morning Colors." The
Stars and Stripes broke out at the island's flagpole and
stayed there for fourteen days of heroic action again incon-
ceivable odds. Major Devereux claims that a very strange
thing happened that morning. The bugler was a young man

named Alvin Waronker. He didn't want to be a bugler but had volunteered for music school because he was slated for duty in Alaska and he hated cold weather. He was not a very good bugler. He had never played "To the Colors" without hitting a sour note—except on the morning of December 8, 1941. That morning every note rang true and clear across the island.

At two minutes before noon, Elrod was patrolling to the north of the island above the cloud cover. A rain squall swept in low over the atoll. Behind it, below the clouds at about 2,000 feet, thirty-six heavy Jap bombers came in from the south. They were almost over the island before they were spotted. There was no radar on Wake, and the noise of the surf covered the sound of the approaching planes.

This first surprise blow was the most disastrous of the sixteen Jap air raids on Wake. The attacking planes flew low over the airstrip, plastering the area around it with 100-pound bombs and lacing it with machine-gun fire. They did not hit the strip; they were saving it for their own use after they took the island.

Seven of the Wildcats on the ground were burned, the eighth damaged. Thirty-four of the fifty-five pilots and mechanics were killed or wounded. A 25,000-gallon tank of gasoline and hundreds of smaller drums went up in flames. Then the Japs divided and attacked the Pan-Am hotel, a clipper in the atoll, and the Marine camp.

It was all over in less than ten minutes, but to top it off, when Elrod came back from patrol and landed, he hit some debris on the runway and damaged his plane. Three-quarters of the Wake air force was knocked out before they went into action.

For the rest of that day and all that night they fought the fires, took care of the wounded, and buried the dead. With the help of civilian construction workers, they labored frantically to build underground shelters for the remaining planes, and a dugout that could be blacked out so that mechanics could work around the clock to repair the two planes that might be put back in service.

When he had a breather, one young Marine read a letter from his girl that had come in on the clipper that morning. It said, "As long as you have to be away, darling, I'm so very, very happy you are in the Pacific where you won't be in danger if war comes."

The next day the Japs did not have it so easy. There was no cloud cover for them to sneak through when they came over, again at noon. Two Marine flyers were aloft on patrol. They attacked the twenty-seven planes, shot one down before they had to break off as their own antiaircraft started to burst around them. The 3" guns got another and sent four more away trailing smoke. But the Japs burned the hospital to the ground, killing most of the sick and wounded. They strafed the civilian camp, inflicting fifty casualties.

That night the Marines labored to move their 3" guns —each weighing eight tons—to new locations and set up dummy wooden guns in their place. They knew that the Japs had spotted the gun sites and would concentrate on them in future attacks.

Sure enough, half of the twenty-six bombers that came over the next day plastered the dummy guns. If the battery had not been moved, it would have been wiped out. Instead, from its new position, it knocked down one bomber.

Hank Elrod did better. He shot down two of the big aircraft with his little Wildcat. To do it he made many fast lunges into the middle of the formation. From the ground they looked like hammer blows at the Japs. From then on he was called Hammering Hank.

After three days of bombing the island the Japs were sure that they had softened it up enough for a landing. They approached with a task force of three cruisers, six destroyers, two submarines, and four transports full of specially trained assault troops. Certainly this should be more than enough to take care of the few Marines who were left. In fact, they were so sure of themselves that the Tokyo radio announced the capture of the island. They were a little too optimistic—they never got near the beach.

The Japs started in before daybreak. The Marines spotted the dim shapes in the predawn darkness and trained their guns on them. Devereux ordered, "Hold your fire." The island lay black and silent as the ships crept in. Devereux knew that the cruisers would mount at least 6″ guns. If he disclosed the locations of his 5″ guns the cruisers could stay out of range of the smaller guns and knock them out.

The ships came closer, opened fire, and swept the island with shells. The Marine gun captains called for permission to open up. Devereux' talker kept repeating, "The Major says hold your fire till you get the word." The leading ship, the Japanese admiral's flagship, was a new light cruiser. It passed the island at 6,000 yards, turned and came back, still firing, at 4,500 yards. The destroyers darted in to join it. The landing troops started to go over the sides of the transports into small boats.

Now Devereux ordered, "Commence firing."

There are conflicting reports on how many ships were sunk that day. Devereux claims nine. The Japs claim two. The official report of the Marine Corps says, "two destroyers sunk without survivors, eight ships badly damaged." Regardless of who is right, the Japs took a severe beating and limped home with their tails between their legs.

One pair of 5″ guns caught the lead cruiser with its fourth salvo. She turned and tried to run. They caught her again with the next salvo. A destroyer raced in to lay a smoke screen to cover the stricken ship. The destroyer was hit in the bow. The cruiser was hit again on the forward turret as it limped into the smoke, listing badly and with steam pouring from gaping holes in her side. Another pair of 5″ guns caught a destroyer with its third salvo, which immediately blew up and sank. The young Marine gunners, elated at their success, stopped shooting and started cheering until Sergeant Henry Bedell, an old China Marine, bellowed, "Knock it off, you guys, and get back to the guns. Whad'ya think this is, a baseball game?" The younger Marines later claimed that the Japs went away because they were afraid of Bedell yelling at them.

The Wildcats had taken off when the batteries opened fire, scouted behind the task force looking for carriers, and then came back to attack. After dropping their first bombs, Elrod and another pilot, Captain Tharin, returned to the island for more. They approached Major Putnam, commander of the flyers.

"Sir," said Elrod, "we'd like permission to attack one of those cruisers."

"With fighter planes?" said Putnam. "You wouldn't have a chance."

"Begging your pardon, sir, but we don't agree."

Putnam laughed. "All right, try it if you want to. But remember we're a little short of planes. Be sure you duck the ack-ack."

"Oh, we will, sir," called the pilots as they raced for their planes.

Elrod and Tharin leaped into their ships and climbed steeply for altitude as they disappeared into the clouds. High over the cruiser they peeled off and screeched down in a power dive almost to smokestack level. Elrod's guns blazed in an effort to drive the antiaircraft crews to shelter. They leveled off and released their bombs.

On the ground, the officers listened to the pilots talk to each other by radio. Tharin's guns had jammed, but he made the dive anyway, cursing the armorer who had loaded his weapons. Through the noise of Elrod's guns they heard him grunt in disgust. Three of the four bombs had missed.

The flyers came back to the field and sat in their planes while armorers swarmed over them, loading the guns and replacing the bombs. Then they took off again for another mad dive through a hail of fire toward the cruiser's deck.

Elrod and Tharin made four suicide runs at the cruiser, dropped sixteen bombs, and scored eight hits. When they left it the cruiser was blazing from stem to stern, and the crew was diving over the side of the ship.

But the Wildcats did not escape unharmed. Elrod's plane was so badly shot up that he could not reach the airstrip. Fighting his controls to stay airborne, he managed to reach the beach, where he crash landed. When Devereux and Putnam ran down to help pull him out of the plane, they found him standing in the water, blood running from a little cut on his cheek. As they walked up the beach, he kept saying, "Honest, fellows, I'm awful sorry about the plane."

It was a big day on Wake, and it wasn't over. When the daily bombers came back, the Wildcats brought down two and the 3″ guns a third. To top it off, another of the flyers, Lieutenant Kliewer, sighted a Jap submarine on the surface during dusk patrol. He dived on it, strafed the deck, and scored two bomb hits. When he circled back, nothing was on the surface but a large oil slick.

The days passed—uneventful days except for the daily bombing attacks, which the Marines now took in stride. Stories and legends built up around some of the men. There was the Deacon. He was a sergeant and a very religious man. He did not smoke, drink, or swear, and he would not permit any of his bunk mates to drink or play cards. There was not much they could do about this because the Deacon was also an ex-heavyweight prize fighter. When he wasn't working or fighting, he read his Bible.

The Deacon manned a .50 caliber machine gun. One day a plane dived directly at his gun. The Jap and the Deacon shot it out, toe to toe. The Jap veered off, his ship in flames. The Deacon said, "God bless you, brother," and swung his gun on another plane.

There was a Private Martin, whose attitude expressed

the way most of the Marines reacted to their critical situation. Every morning he would crawl out of his hole between two coral boulders and sing out, with great good cheer, "Good morning, Sergeant. And I sincerely hope that I can say the same thing tomorrow morning."

When they had time, the Marines listened to the stateside radio telling about their fight. It was the only good news in the United States, and radio announcers made the most of it. The Marines were disgusted at repeatedly being called "that gallant little band" or "those immortal heroes," but they thought things had really gone too far when one announcer referred to Wake as "the Alamo of the Pacific." They remembered what had happened to the defenders of the Alamo.

At about this time some radio announcer reported that Devereux had sent a message which became one of the most widely quoted statements of World War Two. In response to a query from Pearl Harbor as to what the Marines needed, Devereux was supposed to have said, "Send us some more Japs."

It was a good line, but Devereux never said it and has never found out how the story started. To the Marines, this kind of dramatic reporting of the job they were doing was very annoying. As one Marine said, "Anybody that wants it can sure have my share of the Japs we already got."

The aviation mechanics worked miracles to keep the Wildcats in the air, trading parts from wrecked planes so that most of the time they kept four aloft. Then one was hit on the ground and burst into flame. While the fire was licking around its gas tank and the bombs were still falling around them, two mechanics pulled the engine out of it and used it to get another plane in the air.

On December 21 there were two air raids, but one of them was different. It was made by carrier-based dive bombers, a sign that another task force was on the way. On December 22 came the last raid, and in it the Marines lost their last two planes. Hank Elrod and the few remaining pilots and mechanics joined the rest of the Marines as infantry.

Wake was small, but it had a coast line of twenty-one miles on three islands. With less than 400 Marines it could not all be defended. This time the Japs sneaked in at night, about 1.30 on the morning of December 23. They landed at four places, three on Wake Island, one on Wilkes. Their principal landing was made by running in two destroyers, crammed with troops, and ramming them up on the beach.

There was only one gun that could bear on this section of the beach—a 3″ antiaircraft gun, and it was without a crew. Lieutenant Hanna, followed by one Marine, ran to it. On the way, three civilians joined them. They cranked down the long slim barrel of the sky weapon. There were no sights on an aintiaircraft gun. Hanna trained it "Kentucky style"—sighting down the barrel through the open breech. They opened fire—one gun and five men, three of whom had never fired a gun before—against two shiploads of troops.

They were not alone long. Elrod led the aviation Marines—about twenty were left—to form an infantry guard for the gun. Hanna's first shot hit the bridge of the destroyer. The vessel burst into flame. In the light of its blaze the scratch gun crew poured shell after shell into the Jap landing force.

There was a newspaper reporter with the Japs. Later he wrote a book. Here is how he described the fight.

"Out of the darkness in front of us, shells came shrieking like a thousand demons let loose. One shell exploded on the bridge. Several men fell where they stood.

"Clambering down ladders and ropes, we disembarked in great haste. The water was so deep we could hardly walk. Rifle in hand, we desperately fought our way forward. Artillery shells, machine gun bullets, rifle bullets— the resisting fire of the enemy grew to a mad intensity. Lying flat on our faces on the beach at the edge of the sea, we could not wiggle an inch. The enemy's tracer bullets which came flying through the dark looked like a show of fireworks. The enemy's position seemed no more than fifty yards away.

"The bullets began to pass close to our backs. We could not remain thus much longer. It was either death or a charge at the enemy. An inch at a time we crept toward the enemy. Twenty yards before the enemy, we prepared to charge. All at once a rain of hand grenades came hurtling down on us.

" 'Charge,' the commander's voice rang out. We jumped to our feet and charged. Huge shadows which shouted something unintelligible were pierced one after another. One large figure appeared before us to blaze away with a machine gun from his hip the way they do in American gangster films. Somebody went for him with his bayonet and went down together with his victim."

That "gangster" was Hank Elrod putting the final touch

that was "beyond the line of duty" on the fourteen days of combat which won him the Medal of Honor. His citation starts by describing how he attacked a flight of twenty-two planes and shot down two, how he sank the first major warship to be destroyed by small-caliber bombs with a fighter plane. Then he fought with a rifle, picking off Japs in the light of the blazing destroyer.

As the Japs started their charge Elrod grabbed an armful of grenades, leaped on the parapet of sandbags surrounding the gun, and started pitching them like baseballs, screaming defiance at the little yellow men. The Japs fell back, rallied, and came on again. This time Elrod met them with an automatic rifle, firing from the hip. As some fell at his feet he advanced toward the rest. There were over 200 Japs surrounding the gun. One Jap was playing dead. As Elrod stood over him, he turned and fired up at the big flyer. Another Marine jumped forward and bayoneted the Jap—but Hank Elrod was dead.

With daybreak the situation was confused. Japs were ashore in force on Wilke and Wake Islands. The telephone lines had all been cut. Jap flags were flying all over Wilke. All the battery positions were isolated, and there was no word from them. Around the airstrip, about eighty-five Marines and civilians were fighting over 1,000 Japs. Suddenly, at Devereux's position in the command dugout, the long-silent telephone rang. His talker picked it up.

A voice whispered, "There are Japanese in the bushes."

"Who are you?" said the talker.

"There are Japanese in the bushes."

"Who are you? Where are you?"

"There are Japanese in the bushes. There are Japanese in the bushes."

Over and over the monotonous, eerie voice whispered into the telephone. "There are Japanese in the bushes." Then there was a scream. Then silence.

Devereux reported the situation to Navy Commander Cunningham, senior officer on the island.

Cunningham replied, "Well, I guess we better give it to them."

Wake Island was surrendered.

It was a bitter decision for the Marines. Many tough old-timers wept. They were still fighting. They had recaptured Wilkes Island and killed every Jap on it. Hanna's gun was still holding out, down to ten men now, nine of them wounded. The Marines thought they could hold on, could win in the end.

But they could not. It was hopeless. Cunningham's decision was the only sensible one. Even if they defeated the landing force, there were plenty more Japs on the ships, enough, ultimately, to kill every Marine on the island. And with all the planes gone, the Japs did not need to land. They could stay out of range of the 5″ guns and bomb and shell the island out of the ocean.

Back in the States, on the day before Christmas, 1941, the last faint glimmer of hope in the Pacific faded. Wake Island had surrendered.

11

MEDAL IN AN EGGSHELL

IN THE YEARS THAT PASSED between the time that Lieutenant Cushing's torpedo boat was sunk by the exploding *Albermarle* in the Civil War and Lieutenant Jack Kennedy's was sunk by a Japanese destroyer in World War Two, torpedo boats changed a great deal. But one thing did not change—duty on a torpedo boat was still a "suicide" service.

Lieutenant Cushing ended up swimming for his life. So did President Kennedy. Cushing swam a few feet to a swamp. The President swam for days from island to island, seeking help for his crew.

Lieutenant Kennedy did not receive the Medal for the dogged courage that saved the lives of his crew. But his exploit points up the kind of valor that was needed for ordinary day-to-day duty in the torpedo-boat service.

Kennedy was at the wheel of PT109 on a dark night,

cruising around the Solomon Islands in the Pacific. The third officer, George Ross, was in the bow with binoculars. Suddenly Ross turned and pointed into the darkness. At the same moment the man on the forward machine gun called, "Ship at two o'clock."

Kennedy spun the wheel to close with the ship—any vessel in these waters would be Japanese. The PT boat was cruising slowly. Before she could get up speed, the black shape of a Japanese destroyer, knifing through the water at forty knots, loomed out of the darkness, bearing down on the little torpedo boat. There was hardly a crash as its sharp bow cut the PT boat in half. The stern sank. Watertight compartments kept the bow afloat as the destroyer rushed off into the darkness.

Clinging to the bow, Kennedy called the roll. Only four men were aboard. Others answered from the water. Two men did not answer. One of those in the water, an engineer named McMahon, was badly burned. Kennedy's first swim was to bring him aboard.

When dawn broke, the half a boat was still afloat. Around them the men could see several islands. They could also see a Japanese camp on the nearest island and knew that they were surrounded by 10,000 Japs. They lay low, listening to the water gurgling into the leaking compartments as the boat sank lower in the sea.

Knowing that the wreck would soon sink, Kennedy ordered his men to try to swim to a tiny island, so small that there might not be any Japs on it. Those who could not swim clung to a plank that had come loose. Those who could swim pushed it. Kennedy swam the three miles with the strap of McMahon's life jacket in his teeth, using a breast stroke. It took him five hours, during which he probably blessed the coach who had compelled him to practice when he was on the Harvard swimming team.

Kennedy knew that just beyond the next little island was Ferguson Passage, through which the PT boats passed on their nightly patrols. Wrapping a flashlight they had saved in a kapok jacket he swam to the next island. As night fell he swam out into the passage and waited, floating in his life jacket and holding the signal light. He waited until he saw gun flashes beyond the islands—flashes that told him that the boats had gone around the islands instead of through the passage. Then he tried to swim back.

But the tricky current had turned against him, he was swept past the island. He stopped swimming and let himself drift. All night he drifted in a complete circle around two of the Jap-infested islands. With dawn he found himself back where he had started from, but this time the current was with him. His men found the skipper whom they had given up for lost vomiting on the beach. He had been in the water for twenty-four of the last thirty hours.

The men were starting to suffer from thirst. A few miles away was another island that seemed to be uninhabited, but on which there were coconut palms. Followed by his crew, and again towing McMahon with his teeth, Kennedy struck out for the other island. This swim took three hours.

The coconut milk made them sick, but that was better than dying of thirst. That night it rained, but they had nothing in which to catch the rain water. Someone suggested that they lick the water from the leaves of bushes. When daylight came, they saw that the leaves they had been licking were covered with bird droppings. That made them sicker. They christened the spot Bird Island.

On the fourth day Kennedy and Ross swam to another island to explore. This was a short swim—one hour. On the beach they found a box of Japanese candy, some hard-tack, a keg of water, and a one-man canoe. That night Kennedy took the canoe out into Ferguson Passage and waited for PT boats. Again they did not come. With morning he paddled back to Bird Island, and passed out hard-tack and water, and then started back to Ross. On the way, rough water swamped his canoe. He started to swim. Suddenly two South Sea natives appeared from nowhere in a canoe, took him aboard, and paddled him back to Ross.

The natives showed the officers where a two-man canoe was hidden. Kennedy scratched a message on a coconut shell with a knife, gave it to the natives, and said, over and over, "Rendova, Rendova." At last the natives understood. He wanted them to go to Rendova, where the PT boat base was located. They paddled off.

Now there was nothing to do but wait—if the natives got through. But Kennedy was taking no chances. That night he and Ross took the two-man canoe out into Ferguson Passage. Again no PT boats, but a violent storm came up. They clung to the canoe after it was swamped by six-foot waves until they were washed up on a reef, cut and bleeding from the sharp coral. Struggling to shore, they dropped to the sand and slept.

They awoke to see four burly natives staring down at them. One of them said, in perfect English, "I have a letter for you, sir." The letter was from a lieutenant commanding a patrol of New Zealand infantry on New Georgia whom the first two natives had reached. It said that he had radioed their position to Rendova.

That night Kennedy was back in the Ferguson channel, this time in the native war canoe. In the dark he heard the purr of PT boat engines, then four shots. He drew his revolver and answered the signal. The sleek boat came out of the darkness.

A voice called, "Is that you, Jack?"

Lieutenant Kennedy answered, "Where the hell have you been?"

The President's heroism was in the line of duty; he did not receive the Medal. But there was another PT boat skipper who did—Lieutenant Commander John Bulkeley. In addition to the Medal of Honor, he won the Navy Cross, the Army Distinguished Service Cross, an Oak Leaf Cluster in lieu of a second Distinguished Service Cross, the Army Silver Star Medal, a Gold Star in lieu of a second Silver Star, the Legion of Merit, the Army Distinguished Unit Badge, the Purple Heart, twelve service medals or campaign badges, the Republic of the Philippines Distinguished Conduct Star, and the French Croix de Guerre. If Bulkeley has any room left on his uniform, he is also entitled to wear the Expert Pistol Shot Medal and the Expert Rifleman Medal.

In the last months of 1941 Lieutenant Commander Bulkeley commanded Motor Torpedo Boat Squadron Three in the Philippines—six speedboats about seventy feet long, each powered by three Packard marine engines. The MTBs were floating egg shells made of plywood. They had no protective armor; their only protection was speed. Their job was to dash in, deliver a knockout punch, and dart out—if they could. They were fast, but not fast enough to outrace bullets.

Each boat was armed with four torpedo tubes and four .50 caliber machine guns. Even the shields of the guns were plywood; steel would be too heavy. Their only purpose was to keep the spray out of the gunner's eyes and, perhaps, make him feel safer because something was between him and the enemy.

Torpedo boats were no place for sissies even when there was no enemy. At high speed in a rough sea the crew of the little cockleshells took a worse beating than professional football players and came ashore covered with bruises from head to toe from being tossed around in the boat. Hitting anything floating on the surface would tear the bottom out of the frail craft.

Bulkeley and his egg shells were ferried to the Philippines by a tanker late in the fall of 1941. They were in the harbor of Manila when Pearl was attacked and patrolled tensely until December 10, when the first wave of Jap planes struck Manila. The little boats drew blood the first day as they knocked down three Jap dive bombers with their machine guns. But the Japs flattened the naval station at Cavite.

Almost before they went into action the squadron was without a base, without food, without gasoline, without extra torpedoes, and, most important, without parts for their engines. The high-speed engines needed to be overhauled constantly, and they did not even have a spare gasket.

They found a base—some native huts on stilts on the shore of the bay. They collected cans of food from a bombed-out warehouse. They located a fuel barge that the Navy had towed to sea. Later they found that the gasoline had been sabotaged with wax, frequently causing their engines to conk out at the worst possible times.

For the few days before the Japs landed, the little boats ferried wounded and did courier duty around the bay. Then as the Jap fleet closed in and troops landed on the islands, they went into action. A Jap cruiser was blasting American troops on shore at Subic Bay, up the coast from Manila. Bulkeley was told to go get it. He left with two boats, one commanded by Lieutenant DeLong. Here's how he described the action:

"It was darker than hell and the shore was lined with Jap field guns. We had got in a little way when a Jap searchlight spotted us and blinked out a dot-dash challenge. We changed course. A field gun opened up but none of their shells fell near us.

"By this time the Japs on Grande Island realized that something funny was going on. They broke out .50 caliber machine gun fire at us—we could see the tracer bullets. Then the fun started—lights and big shore batteries rambling all over the bay, feeling for us. We could hear the shells whistling over our heads. The lights and flashes really helped us, because they enabled us to pick out the shore line and tell where we were.

"By one o'clock we were where we planned to meet De-Long and go in together for the attack. He didn't show up and there was nothing to do but go in alone. To make the sneak, we rounded Binango Point at idling speed. Everything was quiet—no firing down here. Then we saw the cruiser ahead in the dark not 500 yards away. We crept up

on her and had just readied two torpedoes when a searchlight came on and in dot-dash asked us who we were.

"We answered all right—with two torpedoes. Then I
gave our boat hard rudder and started away; it isn't safe
for an MTB to linger near a cruiser. One of our torpedoes
hit home. Looking back we saw red fire rising, and heard
two more explosions which might have been her maga-
zines.

"But we had no time to look at the fireworks. One of
our torpedoes had failed to get out of its tube and was
stuck there, its propellers buzzing and compressed air hissing so that you couldn't hear yourself think. A torpedo is
adjusted to fire after its propeller has made a certain number of revolutions; after that it is cocked like a rifle and
even a good hard wave-slap would set it off, blowing us
all to glory. Our torpedoman, Martino, used his head fast.
He grabbed a handful of toilet paper, jumped astride that
wobbling, hissing torpedo and jammed the vanes of the
propeller with the toilet paper, stopping it.

"Flames on the cruiser were lighting up the bay behind
us. All over Subic Bay, hell was breaking loose. With mo-
tors roaring and the boat skipping around in the rough
water, I guess we made a considerable commotion. Anyway, the Tokyo radio, reporting the attack the next day,
said that the Americans had a new secret weapon—a mon-
ster that roared, flapped its wings, and fired torpedoes in
all directions. It was only us, but we felt flattered. We got
out of there and that was all there was to it."

The Japs quickly took Manila as the few American and
Philippine troops retreated to Bataan peninsula. All during January and February they fought a desperate action,

retreating slowly down the peninsula ahead of an overwhelming force toward the rock fortress of Corregidor.
During those two bitter months Bulkeley and his little
boats were the only American Navy in the Philippines.

They prowled the water at night, hunting Jap shipping.
They broke up landings and sank landing barges. Once
they spotted an auxiliary aircraft carrier anchored near
shore and started to sneak up on her. Barely in time, they
found that it was a trap. The Japs had left the ship there as
bait and had planted floating entanglements around it to
snag the propellers of the torpedo boats.

It didn't work. Bulkeley skirted the obstructions and
fired a torpedo at 1,000 yards before he was spotted, then
put on speed and dashed in, past his own torpedo, to fire
another at 400 yards. As he swerved to sweep the deck
with machine-gun fire the first torpedo hit, and pieces of
the wrecked vessel hurtled around the speedboat.

Then Bulkeley says, "A Jap battery of three-inch guns
opened up on us from shore, so we executed that naval
maneuver technically known as getting the hell out of
there—swerving, weaving, avoiding those wire nets, and
dodging their artillery shells until we were out of range."

In February they sank another cruiser. This one was
under way. As they closed with it they were caught in its
blinding searchlight. Before they came within torpedo
range the cruiser opened with its 6″ guns. The torpedo
boat roared down the path of the searchlight, bouncing
in the splashes of near misses from the heavy shells. They
tried to douse the light with machine-gun fire. It would
not go out. At 4,000 yards they tried for a long shot, then
fired a second fish—the last on the boat—and veered off.

The cruiser chased them, continuing to fire her 6″ guns, until there was a dull boom. The light went out and the cruiser was no more.

The Jap's contempt for these puny little boats changed to fear and fury. They became more cautious about letting their ships out at night. Bulkeley tried to lure them out. He planted one PT boat in a cove just outside Subic Bay. Then he darted into the bay at full speed, engines roaring, a wide white wake behind the boat. He wanted to be seen, to induce a destroyer to come out and chase him. When it did, he would lead it past the hidden boat and then—powie.

The Japs wouldn't play, wouldn't match a destroyer against these pigmies that were knocking off their cruisers. So if they wouldn't come out, Bulkeley would have to go in. He had spotted a large tanker moored to a dock far up in the bay. He cut down to idling speed to decrease noise and avoid the telltale wake, sneaked close to shore, and let go two torpedoes. Then he left in a hurry, but the Army ashore sat up all night and watched the beautiful fire as the tanker burned and sank.

There were only four torpedo boats now. DeLong's boat had not joined Bulkeley for the attack on the first cruiser because the bottom had been ripped out of it by a coral reef. A second boat had met a like fate. The others had lost most of their speed. The engines were rough, and no amount of tinkering would get them back in shape.

Living conditions had improved somewhat. They had found a goat slaughterhouse with a dry concrete floor. Except for the smell of goat, this made fine quarters. The food situation was not so good. Every day their diet was the same. Pancakes of flour and water for breakfast, no lunch, canned salmon and rice for dinner. They became so sick of this that they shot a tomcat and boiled it. According to Bulkeley, it was quite good—tasted like duck.

In March the Army was pushed off Bataan peninsula and holed up in the fortress on Corregidor, called The Rock. Back home people were sure that The Rock would hold out, they had been told that it was impregnable.

When it was built it was impregnable, but not to the weapons of World War Two. Its old-fashioned antiaircraft guns could not reach high-flying bombers, and The Rock was slowly being chipped away by 1,000-pound bombs. The Army brass knew that when waves of Japs swarmed ashore to scale The Rock not much would be left to stop them, and that this would happen before the crippled Navy was back in shape to bring help.

The commanding general in the Philippines was Douglas MacArthur. President Roosevelt decided that MacArthur's ability as a general and his great knowledge of the Japanese and the Philippines made him too valuable to let him be captured. He was vitally needed to lead the counterattack when it was ready.

First he had to escape from The Rock. There were only two possible ways of getting through the Japs—a submarine or Bulkeley's little boats. With luck, Bulkeley might get him to the island of Mindanao in the southern Philippines, where he could be picked up by a bomber and flown to Australia. MacArthur had heard of Bulkeley; he chose the torpedo boats.

It would be a long haul. With Jap planes overhead and Jap ships all around, they did not dare run during daylight. The trip would take two nights. They picked a cove on the chart in which to hide during the day. Also they strengthened the deck with planks and piled the last of the gasoline aboard in fifty-gallon drums. There were no filling stations on the route.

When MacArthur came aboard, two future Medal winners were on the little boat, both "lieutenants"—Lieutenant Commander Bulkeley and Lieutenant General MacArthur. The Medal may be given to a general commanding armies in the field without a particular act of valor. MacArthur was awarded the Medal for commanding the forces in the Pacific that ultimately compelled the Japanese surrender. This made him the only Medal-winning son of a Medal-winning father. General Arthur MacArthur received the Medal for bravery at Missionary Ridge in the Civil War.

MacArthur did not leave alone. His wife and small son were with him, and seventeen others who were considered the most valuable men on The Rock. These included several generals and an admiral, but the selection was not made on the basis of rank; there were also an Air Force captain and a sergeant, while thirty generals stayed behind.

The trip to Mindanao was uneventful. They lost a third boat at the cove. The boats had become separated during the night. Two arrived at the meeting place. They saw another vessel in the distance and at first thought that it was a Japanese destroyer. One of the torpedo boats jettisoned its extra gasoline so that it would have enough speed to attack. The approaching boat was another of their own, but now one boat did not have enough gas to continue.

Passengers were shifted, and the boat and its crew were left behind.

There was also a storm with twenty-foot waves that made the generals very unhappy—they were deathly seasick. One member of the crew said, "I offered my bunk to one general who was lying on the deck after I'd stepped on him a couple of times in the dark, but he said, 'Son, just leave me—I haven't got the strength to move.'"

Lieutenant Kelley, who commanded one of the boats, had more trouble than the others. He had the Admiral aboard. The Admiral had commanded cruisers, battleships, carriers, but he had never been in a torpedo boat. He was horrified. He asked Kelley to take a bearing on a headland. Kelley held up two fingers at a forty-five-degree angle and sighted through them.

"Haven't you got a pelorus?" asked the Admiral.

"No, sir," replied Kelley.

"I suppose the lead boat has one."

"No, sir."

"Then how do you navigate?"

"By guess and by God," replied Kelley.

The Admiral stayed gamely by the wheel for the entire trip, soaking wet and almost frozen. When it was over he said, "I've sailed every type of ship in the Navy except one of these, and I wouldn't do duty on one of these cockleshells for anything—you can have them."

It was a tough trip, but MacArthur caught his bomber. Now there was another VIP to rescue over on Negros Island—President Quezon of the Philippines. Bukeley dashed over to Negros only to be told that the President had been advised not to risk the trip—there were seven Japanese destroyers in the area. When Bulkeley went to see Quezon the President changed his mind. Bulkeley claimed that His Excellency was impressed by his long black beard—no one had shaved for days. Later, when Quezon saw Bulkeley clean-shaven, he said he never would have gone if he had known that he was riding with a boy.

Back at Mindanao, their rescue work finished, they were down to one serviceable boat. One had dragged its anchor and landed on a reef. Another had ripped a big gash in its hull on the Quezon trip. Bulkeley was determined that he would get what was left of his fleet back in action. He learned that there was a machine shop over on Cebu Island. He went over. Here he met a seventy-one-year-old man from Minnesota named "Dad" Cleveland. Dad ran the machine shop. He listened to Bulkeley's story, then said, "Son, you fight 'em, I'll fix 'em."

One of the two boats was put back in shape. Not very good shape, but it could fight—if they had torpedoes. They got a break. Two submarines came into Cebu to load up with food to take to Corregidor. Bulkeley went to see the submarine skippers and pointed out that they could carry more food if they gave him their torpedoes. He finally coaxed some "fish" out of them—four for each boat.

A supply convoy for The Rock was forming up at Cebu. It was supposed to have air cover, heavy bombers from Australia. But two Japanese destroyers and a heavy cruiser were in the neighborhood. If Bulkeley could take care of the destroyers it would leave only the cruiser for the bombers.

Bulkeley and Kelley took positions in the narrow channel between Cebu and Negros, and lay hidden in the dark.

If both destroyers showed up, Bulkeley was to take the first, Kelley the second. They waited. A black shape came around the point into the channel. It was not a destroyer. It was one of the heaviest cruisers the Japs had.

All was quiet aboard the little boats. The unsuspecting cruiser came on—1,500 yards, 1,000 yards, 500 yards, almost point-blank range. Bulkeley fired two torpedoes. They swerved and straddled the cruiser. Kelley fired. His fish, too, went wide, and now the cruiser was alert. She put on speed and flashed her searchlights around the sky, seeking torpedo planes.

Bulkeley swung in a wide arc around the Jap ship and came in on the other side. He let go his last two torpedoes. This time he scored two hits. Then he dashed under the big ship's stern to draw their fire and give Kelley a chance for another shot.

Kelley came up on the stern quarter and ran into the beam of a searchlight and streams of machine-gun fire. With his own guns blazing, one on the light and the others sweeping the deck to drive off the Jap gunners, he kept coming—he wasn't going to miss again. At 300 yards he let go the last two torpedoes. Both hit home in the cruiser's stern. The giant ship sank in twenty minutes.

At this point the destroyers came up—not two, but four. Three of them chased after Bulkeley, one after Kelley. Bulkeley made a dash for shallow water, where the destroyers could not follow. He got away, but Kelley was not so lucky. Before he could evade the destroyer's light, his boat was caught by a hail of bullets that wounded one man, put his port turret out of action, and shot away his mast.

He too tried for shallow water, but in the dark he ran

aground on coral, puncturing his hull. Before he could get loose, it was morning. As he tried to limp home in daylight with his leaking vessel, he was caught in the open by four Jap bombers.

Standing at the wheel with his eyes on the bombers, Kelley watched until he saw a bomb start to fall. Then he threw the wheel hard over to dodge it. He did this until the Japs had dropped all their bombs without scoring a hit. Then the planes started to dive on the little craft, spraying it with machine-gun fire. This was more effective. The boat's gunners shot down one plane, but the other three planes killed one and wounded several of the crew, and knocked out the rest of the guns and one engine.

His boat sinking under him, Kelley made a run for the beach. The crew got away, carrying their dead and wounded, but now there was only one boat.

That was the last fight for Motor Torpedo Boat Squadron Three. When Bulkeley got back to Mindanao he found an order: no more gas for torpedo boats; all that was left was needed for planes. Then he received another order, from MacArthur. The General was so impressed with the PT boats that he wanted experienced officers sent back to the States to train more crews. Bulkeley was ordered to fly to Australia. Ultimately three of the other officers were taken off before the Philippines fell.

Bulkeley fought again, commanding PT boats in the English Channel when Americans landed in France to conquer Hitler. But the epic of MTB Squadron Three was over. Or not quite over. There was one boat left.

There is a lake on Mindanao Island, Lake Lanao. If it could be defended from Japanese seaplanes, American flying boats could land here after the airfields were lost. The last of the PT boats was hauled overland by water buffalo to serve as a gunboat on the lake. Chugging around on fresh water was a sad end for the dashing, daring, seagoing PT boat, but it was still fighting.

12

MEDALS IN THE ISLANDS

Palm trees swaying in the lazy trade winds against an azure sky. Sparkling surf rolling up beaches of soft, gleaming sand. Smiling native girls swinging supple hips in an island dance. That's what the South Sea Islands were like—little bits of paradise. Everybody knew that. Hollywood had told them. Everybody had seen Bob Hope and Bing Crosby singing to Dorothy Lamour wearing a sarong in such surroundings.

In 1942 several hundred thousand young Americans started to learn that Hollywood had lied to them. The South Sea Islands were not little bits of paradise. They were big chunks of hell. The swaying palm trees were dense, steaming jungles. The soft white sand was sharp, jagged coral. The smiling native girls were snakes and rats and fever-carrying mosquitoes. There were rugged little mountains honeycombed with caves. And the caves and the coral and the jungles were filled with fanatical little Japs who had to be blasted out, burned out, shot out, or bayoneted out in the long march back.

After Pearl Harbor it was six months to the day before there was any good news from the Pacific. Then Communique Number 77 started with the sentence, "Very excellent news has been received." The groggy Navy had recovered and stopped a Japanese invasion force in the Coral Sea off the coast of Australia. A month later they broke the back of Jap carrier strength in the naval battle of Midway. The march back had started.

But it's a long way from Australia to Japan, a route filled with island steppingstones. Americans started to fumble with the pronunciation of island names like Guadalcanal, Bougainville, Kwajalein, Eniwetok, Tarawa, and Peleliu as American, Australian, and New Zealand forces, spearheaded by the Marines, recaptured island after island on the long road to Tokyo.

Seventy-nine Marines won the Medal in this island fighting. Here self-sacrifice was still the keynote of the awards. Twenty-seven of the Marines—more than one third of the Medal winners—gained the Medal by deliberately falling on Japanese hand grenades to save their comrades by absorbing the force of the exploding grenades with their own bodies.

There is a monotony of inspired heroism in reading these citations. That of Corporal Charles Berry says:

". . . he engaged in a pitched hand grenade duel, returning the dangerous weapons with prompt and deadly accuracy until an enemy grenade landed in the foxhole. Determined to save his comrades, he unhesitatingly chose to sacrifice himself and dived on the deadly missile, absorbing the shattering violence of the exploding charge in his own body."

Corporal Anthony Damato ". . . lay with two comrades in a large foxhole in his company's defense perimeter. When one of the enemy approached the foxhole undetected and threw in a hand grenade, Corporal Damato groped for it in the darkness. Realizing the imminent peril to all three and fully aware of the consequences of the act, he flung himself on the grenade and, although instantly killed as his body absorbed the explosion, saved the lives of his two companions."

Private William Foster ". . . absorbed the exploding charge in his own body, thereby protecting the other Marine from serious injury. Although mortally wounded as a result of his heroic action he quickly rallied, handed his own remaining two grenades to his comrade and said, 'Make them count.' "

Private Henry Gurke ". . . mindful that his comrade manned an automatic weapon of superior fire power and therefore could provide more effective resistance, thrust him roughly aside and flung his own body over the missile to smother the explosion."

Lieutenant Robert Rouh ". . . quick to act in spite of his weakened condition, he lurched to a crouching position and thrust both men aside placing his own body between them and the grenade and taking the full blast of the explosion himself."

Twenty-four of the twenty-seven awards for falling on grenades end with the words "He gallantly gave his life for his country."

The heroism of these men is beyond understanding. Put yourself in their place. You are crouched in a shell hole. A live grenade drops in. What would you do? Almost certain death is laying at your feet. Every instinct says, "Run —duck—hide." If you had more than average valor you might go toward the grenade, try to throw it out.

In a split second these men realized there wasn't time to throw it out. They knew that death would explode in that foxhole the next instant. Either all would be killed or one would be killed. Their devotion to their duty and their cause was so great that it overcame every instinct for self-preservation and led them to choose almost certain death so that their comrades could fight on.

Volunteering for death-defying missions was common practice when Americans had their backs to the wall in the Pacific. One such mission began at a restaurant table in Washington. A lieutenant colonel and a general were sitting at the table. The colonel was marking up the table-cloth with figures as he earnestly argued and pleaded with his commander. For two hours the general said, "No." Finally he gave in and said, "Yes." He gave Lieutenant Colonel James Doolittle permission to bomb Tokyo, a feat for which he was awarded the Medal.

If Tokyo was to be bombed, General "Hap" Arnold could not have found a better man to do it than Jimmy Doolittle. He had been a flyer for twenty-five years, was a World War One pilot. His main fame was based on winning air races. He won almost every trophy that was put up during the 1920s and 1930s. That made him a daredevil. But Jimmy Doolittle also had a doctor's degree in aeronautical engineering from M.I.T. He could take a plane up, win a race, bring it down, take it apart, and explain to the scientists in the laboratory just what had happened to it under extreme conditions.

If any planes were to get to Tokyo in April, 1942, it would take a man with this combination of qualities to get them there. The Navy had no planes that were big enough for the job. The Army had no bases that were near enough for even their longest-range bombers. Jimmy's idea was to use Army bombers, twin-engine B25s, and take off from a carrier.

This had never been done. Presumably it could not be done because the carrier deck was not long enough for such a heavy plane. Doolittle said it could be done. Of course, the planes could not land on a carrier. They would have to fly on over Japan to fields in the interior of China— fields behind the coastal area that was occupied by the Japs.

The word went out for volunteer crews to man twenty-four B25s for a mission that was "important and interesting —and dangerous." Nobody knew what the mission was, but the planes from all over the country started to arrive at remote Elgin Field, in Florida.

The Army flyers got their first hint at the nature of their mission when the Navy lieutenant showed up to train them in quick take-offs. An area 500 feet long was marked off on a little secret field near Elgin, and they practiced taking off in a shorter distance than it was thought possible to take off with a B25—take-offs at sixty or seventy miles an hour with the flaps all the way down instead of at eighty or ninety miles an hour.

They practiced low-level flying, skipping along the wave tops in the gulf of Mexico. They practiced bombing from

500 feet, raising bumps on their heads when the concussion of the bursting bombs threw them against the top of the cabin. They practiced navigation out over the Gulf. Whatever their mission, they now knew it would be over water.

Still it was a surprise and a shock when they were ordered to a little field on the California coast and came in over the aircraft carrier *Hornet* at a nearby wharf. Everybody had the same comment, "Gee, ain't she small."

Sixteen of the planes were swung aboard the *Hornet* with a crane. Surrounded by a task force of cruisers and destroyers, the *Hornet* started its long dash across the Pacific, destination unknown.

But not unknown for long. The first day out, Doolittle briefed the men.

"We are going straight to Japan. We're going to bomb Tokyo, Yokohama, Osaka, Kobe, and Nagoya. The Navy is going to take us in as close as advisable, and, of course, we're going to take off from the deck. The Chinese government will cooperate with us. We've made complete arrangements to land at small Chinese fields where gas is waiting for us. We'll tank up and fly on to Chungking."

Doolittle then performed a little ceremony. Several Navy officers had received medals from the Japanese government in the past. Now these medals were tied to the noses of bombs. They were being sent back to the Japs.

The whole operation seemed quite simple the way Doolittle had it figured out—that is, it would be simple if the planes could get off the carrier deck. They were supposed to make the bombing run on the night of April 19, probably would not meet antiaircraft fire or fighters because of the surprise. So far as the Japs knew, the nearest big bombers were 3,000 miles from their homeland.

But it did not work out that way. On the morning of April 18 battle stations sounded. As the men raced for their planes the guns of nearby cruisers crashed out. Near the horizon they could see black smoke billowing from a sinking ship. It was a Japanese patrol boat.

The Navy sank it in three minutes, but it had time to signal the location of the task force. In these waters Japan probably had naval strength that could destroy the little task force with ease. They were still 800 miles from the Japanese coast, instead of 400 miles, the planned take-off point. The ships would have to turn back; they were too valuable to take such a risk.

The planes could easily reach Tokyo from this point, but they could not reach the Chinese inland fields where gas was waiting or any other airfields. In a split-second decision, Doolittle decided to take off anyway for a daylight run. They had come to bomb Tokyo and they would bomb Tokyo. What happened after, they would worry about later. The daredevil in Doolittle took over from the scientific planner.

The *Hornet* turned into the wind and started steaming under forced draft. Doolittle lined his plane up on the white line painted on the outer edge of the carrier deck. The big B25s could not take off down the center of the deck but had to make the run with one wing hanging over the edge of the ship so that the other wing would clear the carrier's control tower.

At the forward end of the deck a Navy officer waited with signal flags. He was an expert at timing the pitch of the ship so that a plane would reach the end of the deck as the bow was lifted by a wave. Doolittle waited, engines running at top speed, brakes jammed on. The signalman dropped his flag. Sailors snatched the chocks from in front of the plane's wheels. Doolittle's plane lumbered forward along the white line, the howling wind pushing against his down-thrust flaps. As he neared the bow of the ship it rose on a perfectly timed wave. When it dropped, the ship was air-borne.

One after another the planes took off without mishap, circled the carrier to get a bearing for the heart of Japan, and started their long flight. They flew in single file, fifteen or twenty feet above the wave tops. They mushed along slowly to get the best mileage from every drop of gas.

The trip was tense but uneventful. In addition to an auxiliary tank each plane carried ten five-gallon cans of gas. They topped the tanks from these as they flew along. At about 2.00 P.M. they sighted the low-lying coast of Japan, increased their speed, and flew along at housetop level.

They met no resistance. Doolittle described people run-ning out to wave at them. The red center of the Army wing insignia was not unlike the red "rising sun" emblem on Japanese planes. They continued at roof-top level, where antiaircraft could not reach them, flew over a school where they could see the little slant-eyed faces of children in the yard, flew over a baseball park and broke up the game, flew over neat little farms and cherry trees in bloom.

They hopped over a range of mountains, flew down a valley, crossed another range, and there, across Tokyo Bay, was Japan's capital—the place that the Japanese Emperor, the Son of Heaven, had said that the white men would never reach.

Over the city the planes zoomed up to 1,500 feet, and each went for its preassigned targets—factories, shipyards, refineries. Each plane had three 500-pound high-explosive bombs and an incendiary bomb. Then they dropped back down and streaked for the China Sea. Some planes were attacked by fighters, some met antiaircraft fire; but none was shot down, and no one was hurt over Japan.

It was another 1,200 miles to the safe Chinese airports. They knew that they would never make it. They droned along toward the China coast, hit it at dusk, and kept on, hoping to get beyond the Japanese-occupied coastal area before they had to ditch their planes and jump.

As the gas gauges bumped the bottom they readied chutes. At about 10.00 P.M. Doolittle realized that he was as near unoccupied China as he was going to get. He ordered his crew to jump. Then, flashlight in hand, he dived out the door into the rainy night, somewhere over the part of China held by friendly Chinese—he hoped.

Doolittle made out well in his jump. He landed in a nice, soft, freshly plowed field. It had been freshly fertilized too, and they don't use four footed animal manure for fertilizing in China. He didn't come out "smelling like a rose," but he came out in one piece, and he was, by a very slight margin, past the Japanese area.

Some of the other men did not make out so well. Only one plane landed safely, in Siberia, where the Russians interned the crew. One man was killed when his chute did not open. Two planes landed among the Japanese.

The crews were not treated as prisoners of war. They were tried as bandits and executed.

Most of the flyers landed in territory occupied by the Japs but were rescued by friendly Chinese, who led them to safety after hair-raising adventures. One plane crash-landed in the water, injuring all but one of the crew. These men were cared for by Chinese guerrillas, peasants, and missionaries as they were passed on to safety—sometimes on Chinese junks, sometimes in sedan chairs, sometimes on the backs of coolies. The pilot was seriously injured. His leg had to be amputated. In some mysterious way the Chinese, through a peasant grapevine, found the party's doctor, who was with the crew of another plane, and led him to the injured pilot. He cut the leg off in the living room of a missionary, by lamp light, assisted by an old Chinese doctor.

Doolittle's raid did not hurt the Japs much. The damage that was done was soon repaired. But the courage of the man who led it—far "beyond the call of duty"—brought new hope to the American people in those dreary spring days of 1942 and carried a message of fear of things to come to the victory-confident Japanese.

13

MEDALS IN RETREAT

SERGEANT KENNEMORE WAS HUNGRY. Sergeant Kennemore was cold. Sergeant Kennemore was disgusted. He had food, but he couldn't eat—it was frozen hard as a brick. He had a sleeping bag, but in this raw, damp, twenty-degree-below-zero cold it might as well have been a cotton sheet.

And all this suffering was so useless; that's why he was disgusted. This wasn't a war. The United States was at peace with everybody. They didn't even call it a war. It was a police action. Ten years before, when he had joined the Marines, he had sworn to fight to defend the Constitution of the United States; but he hadn't agreed to police a bunch of Gooks in these God-forsaken frozen mountains 5,000 miles from home.

Shivering and grousing, Sergeant Kennemore dozed off. In his sleep he heard bugles and cymbals and whistles. He was dreaming of war. Suddenly one bugle was loud and clear. Sergeant Kennemore was awake. He wasn't dreaming. Easy Company, out there in the cold dark, was under attack.

He scrambled out of his sleeping bag and rushed up the hill toward his section of machine guns. They were firing now, stuttering in the dark. As he reached the crest of the ridge he saw a swirl of dim white figures around one of the guns, jabbing with bayonets. The other gunner was kneeling behind his gun, spraying the corridor that was their field of fire.

The trip flares that they had set in front of their position went off. In the eerie light he saw them. Wave after wave of hunched-over, white-coated men shuffling toward him. The gun mowed down the whole front rank. But others kept coming, rank after rank after rank. Maybe the boot who had asked him, "Sarge, how many hordes are there in a Chinese platoon?" hadn't been so stupid.

Other guns blazed into action—machine guns, carbines, automatic rifles. Mortars in the rear started to cough; their 60 mm. shells plopped among the ghostly attackers. Kennemore threw his carbine to his shoulder. It fired once and died. Automatic weapons did not work well in this weather. He dropped his gun, scrambled on the ground, crawling from body to body, friend and foe alike, seeking grenades. Standing among the corpses he started to throw American pineapple grenades, Chinese potato-masher grenades.

The big Sergeant was the center of a little group now. Others were firing or throwing or running forward to plunge a bayonet into a white figure. The enemy paused and threw a barrage of grenades. Sweating in the cold, Kennemore bent, grabbed a potato masher before it exploded, threw it back—and another, and another, and another. Then one landed just out of reach. He couldn't bend to pick it up in time. Instead he put his big foot on it, jammed it into the snow. The grenade exploded.

The "police action" was over for Sergeant Kennemore, and back in the States a Medal of Honor waited for the legless Marine. It was November, 1950. The fighting had been going on for six months. But it had really started back in 1945.

When small children want to divide things, they sometimes do it with a singsong chant: "One for me, one for you, one for me, one for you." When they get older, they may divide into teams by using a baseball bat, the one who gets his hand nearest the top getting first pick.

In 1945, if the governments of the United States and the U.S.S.R. had used some such simple method of division, a bloody war might have been averted, although that is not likely. If the Russians did not have one excuse for taking over in North Korea they would have found another.

Russia was an ally of the United States in the war against Germany but a neutral in the war against Japan until two days after the atom bomb was dropped on Hiroshima. Then when it was obvious that the fighting was almost over, Russia declared war on Japan. She wanted a share of the spoils.

When Japan surrendered a few days later, Russia had already dashed into Manchuria and northern Korea, which had been occupied by Japan since 1910. The Americans were in South Korea. Solely to determine which Japs should surrender to which country's troops, it was decided that all forces north of the thirty-eighth parallel of latitude should surrender to the Russians and all those south of that line to the Americans.

This was supposed to be a temporary arrangement to divide prisoners. The Russians did not see it that way. They were in and they intended to stay in. In 1948 the United Nations ordered that an election be held in Korea. The Russians would not let the North Koreans vote. South Korea elected a government. The Russians had a so-called election of their own in North Korea and put in a Communist government. Now there were two Koreas.

The Americans went home. The Russians supposedly went home, but they would not let anyone in to check whether they had. Before they left, the Americans set up a South Korean Army, trained and equipped it as a police force armed only with small infantry weapons. The Russians set up a North Korean Army, trained and armed it for aggressive warfare with heavy artillery and large Russian tanks.

On June 25, 1950, the North Korean Army slashed into South Korea and drove the lightly armed South Koreans pell-mell down the peninsula. The United Nations voted to come to the aid of the South Koreans. By the time the United Nations troops, mostly American, reached Korea in force, the South Koreans and the few Americans who had been airlifted in were holding on by their eyelashes to only the southern tip of the peninsula.

The United Nations troops were a police force sent to control this little local civil war. No one expected it to last long after the Americans arrived. A couple of divisions of well-armed troops should be enough to chase the North

Koreans back where they belonged. Actually the war lasted three long, bloody years. In it, 123 Americans won the Medal of Honor.

At first it seemed as though the optimists were right. The Army started up the peninsula. The Marines landed up the coast at Inchon behind the Communists. The two forces squeezed the North Koreans between them. By the end of October the North Korean Army was no more. Over half the original force had surrendered, and the rest were fleeing up the peninsula with the Americans following them to mop up.

This was the situation when the First Marine Division, including Sergeant Kennemore, landed at Wonsan late in October, well up north on the east coast of Korea. The Marines were not happy about being there. Fighting was their business, but there was no more fighting. Everybody knew the war was over. The first people they met when they came ashore were Bob Hope and a bunch of pin-up girls. The Marines liked the pretty girls, but they felt a little foolish making a landing behind the U.S.O.

What the Marines did not know, what commanding General Douglas MacArthur over in Tokyo did not know, was that across the Yalu River, in Manchuria, which borders Korea on the north, were three tough, well-equipped armies of Chinese Communists who were about to take a hand in the fighting.

MacArthur ordered an all-out advance to the Yalu River to end the war. The American Eighth Army was to go up the west side. The Tenth Corps, headed by the First Marines, was to go up the east coast, turn inland at Hung-nam, and head for the Chosin reservoir seventy-eight miles away along a narrow road flanked by mountain ridges. As the Eighth Army reached the Yalu and the Marines reached the reservoir, the Chinese struck.

Two of the Chinese armies sent the Eighth Army reeling back down the peninsula. The third turned east to pinch off the Marines strung out on the narrow road between the coast and the reservoir. The Chinese had no tanks, no heavy guns—only rifles, bazookas, machine guns, and grenades. They did not seem dangerous, these little yellow coolies in their padded cotton coats and canvas tennis shoes, each carrying a bag of rice.

Their lack of heavy weapons and the fact that they did not have to depend on supply lines made them dangerous. By night they padded through mountain passes at a dog-trot. By day they holed up in Korean huts, munching their rice. Soon 100,000 of them had reached the high ground above the road. The 20,000 Marines did not know that these tough veterans, battle hardened from the Communist victory in China, were all around them.

Two regiments of Marines were at Yudam-ni. The third was divided between Hagaru, fourteen miles down the road, and Kotori, eleven miles farther back. The Chinese struck the road between the towns and set up roadblocks to separate the three groups. Then they attacked at Yudam-ni. That's where Sergeant Kennemore got it.

For three nights the Marines beat back attack after attack. They were always the same. Out of the still dark would suddenly sound the crash of cymbals, the blare of bugles, the shrill squeal of whistles. Then white figures by the thousands would charge through the snow, chanting in English, "Kill Marines, Marines die. Kill Marines, Marines die."

With each dawn the ground was covered with Chinese dead. During the day the Marines improved their defenses, using frozen Chinese bodies for breastworks when sand-bags were scarce. But next night there were thousands more chanting Chinese to be mowed down.

It was clear to Major General Howard Smith, com-manding the First Division, that he could not go forward and that he could not stay where he was, strung out on the road. He would have to pull back his leading regiments and fight his way down the road to the sea. Back at head-quarters in Tokyo they had already written off the First Division. They were completely surrounded. The Eighth Army had been driven far back, leaving the Marines alone in the mountains to the north.

The "retreat from the reservoir" is one of the greatest epics in Marine Corps fighting history, but it makes Marines mad to hear it called a retreat. General Smith carefully explained that a retreat is an orderly retirement to the rear. But the First Division had no rear; they were surrounded. "So," explained Smith, "We are not retreat-ing. We are merely attacking in another direction."

Between Yudam-ni and Hagaru is Toktong Pass. The hill above it had to be held while the two leading regiments fought their way down to Hagaru. It is called Fox Hill because it was defended by Fox Company of the Seventh Marines under Captain William Barber. Among the 240 men in Fox Company was Private Hector Cafferata—six foot four, 235 pounds, ex-semiprofessional football player.

At 2.00 A.M. on the morning of November 28 Private

Cafferata was asleep in his bag with his shoes off. Captain Barber was awake in his command post. He did not know it, but the Chinese had cut the road on both sides of his position. A full regiment of them were surrounding his hilltop. When they captured this hill they would have complete command of the road at this point. The two regiments at Yudam-ni would be doomed.

Cafferata woke to the sound of guns blazing up ahead and came charging out of his foxhole. He saw the white shapes coming toward him, threw his rifle to his shoulder, calmly squeezed off shot after well-aimed shot until the Chinese recoiled from this deadly giant standing barefoot in the snow. A dozen dead Chinese lay in front of him before his frozen rifle quit.

He jumped into another foxhole, where a Marine lay wounded, and shouted, "Gimme a rifle." The wounded Marine passed up his and reached for the weapon of a dead buddy to reload while Cafferata fired. Standing on the edge of the hole, he used two rifles to clear the ground in front of him of living Chinese.

Cafferata was the only man left at this point in the line. He ran back and forth, trying to seem like a squad. The Chinese dropped to the ground and started to lob grenades. Cafferata kicked them aside as he ran, caught one, and threw it back. It exploded as it left his hand, blowing off his little finger.

Other Marines rallied around him, some using entrenching tools to bat back the grenades before they landed. From the rear, mortars zeroed in on the Chinese. With dawn the Communists fell back, leaving the snow-covered slope littered with white-clad bodies. Now there were only scattered pockets of resistance. One of these was a machine gun. Cafferata charged it. He felt a searing pain in his arm and shoulder and chest. He fell and crawled back toward his lines. When his buddies picked him up they saw that he had fought in the snow for five hours—and won the Medal of Honor—in his bare feet.

Night came again to Fox Hill—night and more squat Chinese blowing their off-key bugles, clanging their brazen cymbals, chanting their song of death. In front of their position the Marines had arranged a clever ruse—a circle of sleeping bags filled with snow in the path of fire of their machine guns. The Chinese who stopped to bayonet the sleeping snow men fell in lasting sleep under the rain of machine-gun fire.

Captain Barber moved along his front line. He fell to the ground. A bullet had passed through both legs. He called to a Marine to hold him up and hobbled along the line on his wounded legs. He was hit again. Still he kept fighting. With dawn, the Chinese again withdrew. Fox Hill was still holding out, but the 240 Marines were down to 120.

Another night. Barber had tried tying boards to his legs to keep them from crumpling under him. It worked for a while. Then he commanded from a stretcher carried along the line. The third Chinese attack was beaten off,— but now there were only about eighty Marines left.

On December 1, the two regiments at Yudam-ni prepared to pull back. They buried their dead, loaded their wounded on trucks, and started down the road. To relieve Fox Hill and secure Toktong Pass, Lieutenant Colonel Davis struck out into the mountains with a battalion, making a wide circle around the roadblocks. There were two mountain peaks held by the Chinese between him and Barber.

He could not take vehicles or heavy weapons. Two mortars and six machine guns were carried on the men's backs. Shells were carried in stretchers. In single file the battalion crept forward in the dark through knee-deep snow and bitter cold. Men lurched and fell; some had to be kicked to their feet—it would be so much easier to lie there and peacefully freeze to death.

They lost direction in the dark. The radio went dead. Davis tried to navigate by the stars, but in the ravines he could not see the stars. He fumbled with his compass and flashlight, then floundered to the head of the column to push it in the right direction. He was behind the Communists on the first mountain peak now. The mortars were set up. The machine guns opened on the startled Chinese. The Marines lumbered up the steep slope and reached the summit to bayonet the last of the enemy.

The men slumped in the snow and tried to eat their frozen rations. Officers and noncoms passed among them to keep them awake. Two men went crazy that awful night. They were strapped to stretchers in improvised strait jackets and carried forward. With dawn, the Marines buried their dead, then opened fire on the second mountain peak. Carrying their wounded, they charged down the opposite slope, up the second peak, and cleared it of Chinese.

They could see Fox Hill now and the Marines on it. Suddenly the radio came to life. It was Barber calling from his stretcher.

"Do you want me to send a patrol out to help you?"

Laughing and cheering, Davis's men dashed across the valley and up Fox Hill. The two forces united. Barber and Davis watched the two regiments from Yudam-ni pass below them, neither knowing then that he would receive the coveted Medal for the fight on Fox Hill.

Down at Hagaru, part of the remaining regiment was surrounded. When the Chinese first attacked, the only troops available to man East Hill, overlooking the town, were about 200 Army Engineers, half of them South Koreans, many of whom did not even know how to fire a carbine. The Chinese quickly pushed them off the hill and prepared to sweep down to the heart of the American position.

Major Reginald Myers collected what Marines he could find—clerks, orderlies, truck drivers, cooks. He started toward East Hill, picking up a few of the routed Army Engineers on his way. His scratch company crawled up the hill in the face of a full battalion of Chinese. Machine guns cut them down. Grenades bounced down the slope to explode among them. The men took cover, pinned down. Myers rushed from one end of the line to the other, prodding the men on.

His force dwindled, but the Major seemed to bear a charmed life. They approached the crest of the hill—seventy-five of the 300 who had started up. They could not reach the top. But the Chinese could not pass that thin line below the crest. For three days Myers held grimly on to earn the Medal by holding the enemy out of Hagaru until the two regiments rolled into the town behind him.

General Smith ordered Colonel "Chesty" Puller to send what men he could spare from Koto-ri up to Hagaru.

Puller scraped together about 900 men and a few tanks.
It was called Task Force Drysdale because it was led by
Lieutenant Colonel Douglas Drysdale, of the British Royal
Marines. Behind the Royal Marines came a company of
American Marines under Captain George Sitter. The
Marines of the two countries were fighting side by side for
the first time since the Boxer Rebellion. Completing the
column was a U.S. Army company and a hodgepodge
company of clerks, truck drivers, and other usually non-
combat troops.

For nine miles ahead of them the road was flanked by
two divisions of Chinese well entrenched on the heights
and behind roadblocks—over 15,000 men against less than
1,000.

Jaunty in their berets, the Royal Marines led off and
attacked the first roadblock. While they blasted the Chinese
out of the way, the American Marines leapfrogged them
and pushed up the road to drive the enemy from the
next flanking hill. While they mopped up, the Royal
Marines leapfrogged to the front again. Slowly the two
companies of Marines fought their way forward, taking
turns in the lead, the rest of the column inching along
behind.

About four miles up the road the column ground to a
halt. A tank that had scouted ahead came back to report
that the road was impassable. A point up ahead was flanked
by two steep hills. Chinese by the thousands were massed
in ambush on the hillsides. Tanks and infantry on foot
might make it; trucks never could. Taking only a few
trucks for the wounded, the two companies of Marines

and a few soldiers pushed on while the rest of the column turned back.

They reached Hagaru—some of them. It took them sixteen and a half hours to fight every step of the way for those nine miles. Private William Baugh was one who did not make it. When a grenade landed in the truck in which he was riding he threw himself on it. He died and became a Medal winner.

Captain George Sitter received the Medal too for his part in leading the leapfrogging relief column from Koto-ri.

While the Marines were holding at Yudam-ni the engineers had worked a miracle at Hagaru by blasting and scraping an airstrip in the frozen ground to the tune of Chinese bullets pinging off the blades of their bulldozers. As the regiments regrouped at Hagaru planes flew in, brought a few more men, and took out over 4,300 wounded and many dead bodies.

The Air Force offered to fly out the rest of the division. General Smith refused, saying, "We marched in and we'll march out like Marines—taking every piece of our equipment." The 10,000 who were left at Hagaru started the march to Koto-ri, blasting their way through 40,000 fresh troops that the Chinese had thrown in.

At Koto-ri the division was united. But here it seemed that they would have to abandon their vehicles, leave the road, and find their way through the mountains on foot. Three miles below Koto-ri was a deep chasm. The Chinese had blown up the only bridge across it. Rebuilding it on the spot was impossible.

The engineers and the Air Force had an answer. They

built a bridge on the coast, flew it in, and dropped it at the site of the old bridge by parachutes. Each section that floated to earth weighed over two tons.

The First Division came down to the sea on December 10, came down with every truck, every jeep, every gun, and with the frozen bodies of their dead lashed to gun barrels. They had sustained 7,500 casualties, but they had smashed an army of ten or twelve divisions and had inflicted perhaps 37,500 casualties. They were ready to fight again in the new war that had started with the Chinese— ready to fight right away. Painted on the side of one of their tanks was the gay challenge, "Only 14 more shooting days until Christmas."

During the century that the Medal of Honor has been in existence, perhaps fifty million men have served in the armed forces of the United States, a few as life-long professionals, most as civilians turned into fighting men to repel a challenge to liberty. Of these many millions, only 3,155 have won the Medal of Honor—2,190 soldiers and airmen, 728 sailors, 235 Marines, and one Coast Guardsman. It has been awarded to one civilian by special act of Congress. Charles Lindbergh got it for making the first nonstop transatlantic plane flight.

What kind of men are these few who, out of many millions, have reached the very peak of the pyramid of honor? Some of them were old men; some were boys in their early teens. Some were rich; some were poor. Some were native Americans; some were foreign born. Some were white; some were colored. Some were Christians; some were not. When it comes to honor, the greatest virtue that a man can have, no one kind of a man is any better than any other kind.

Bravery is something that can be within anyone, regardless of age, or nationality, or color, or religion. A man is not born to it. He does not have to learn it. The men who are the bravest of the brave have but one thing in common. They are willing to put their duty to their country or the welfare of their comrades above their love for themselves. These are America's greatest heroes—the men, living and dead, whose names are inscribed on the roll of the Medal of Honor.

Date Due